Hacking

Digital Media and Society Series

Mark Deuze, *Media Work*
Alexander Halavais, *Search Engine Society*
Robert Hassan, *The Information Society*
Tim Jordan, *Hacking*
Jill Walker Rettberg, *Blogging*

Contents

Acknowledgements

Thanks to Andrea Drugan and her team who suggested looking at hacking in a series about digital media. Andrea and Jonathan Skerrett were very helpful during writing and production. Several anonymous reviewers offered suggestions which made significant improvements. I drew on years of discussion with far too many people to mention, thanks to all of them. Of course, all mistakes are my own.

To hacking, god knows what I owe in general, but specifically this was written using OpenOffice, operating system Ubuntu. For less specific but nonetheless more important support, thanks to Masters Lite at Clissold Swimming Club and the Ancient Shadows. For the most important things in life, thanks to Matilda and Joanna, though the adventure has been more mountainous while writing this book than I could have expected.

CHAPTER ONE

The Hack

Introducing hacking

The hack is a way of understanding what is possible, sensible and ethical in the twenty-first century. This overview of hacking will explain those who hack and their communities, because only by grasping hacking in the full sense of the people who hack and the social and cultural relations within which they live can we open up some important facets of twenty-first-century life. Further, only by exploring the norms and cultures found in this community will we open up a side to our existence that has arrived – whether we like it or simply put up with it or hate it – with the growing ubiquity of computers and the ever-expanding connections produced by computer networks.

Kevin Mitnick is a hacker, though some would demand he be called a cracker. He became famous for a number of activities: being held responsible for breaking the security on a US government computer security advisor's system, using a technique (IP-spoofing) that had not been documented before; for breaking into the corporations Fujitsu, Motorola, Nokia and possibly others, seeking software for mobile phones to try and secure his own systems; and, for being the hacker who was held in solitary confinement because someone claimed he could launch nuclear weapons by whistling phone tones down a phone line (Shimomura 1995; Littman 1996). Mitnick subsequently became a computer security consultant.

Linus Torvalds is a hacker. He became famous for leading the development of an operating system called Linux. This complex software package began as a technical exercise for Torvalds, who wrote and released the core component (the kernel) of an operating system. Subsequently, Torvalds oversaw an expanding collective effort to write more and more components of it, until Linux emerged as a free, sophisticated operating system which is considered by many to be a technically significant rival to Microsoft's Windows operating system.

Torvalds and Mitnick exemplify the two core components of hacking: cracking, and free software and open source programming. Between these components are generated dynamics which create the particular characteristics of hacking, but these two are not the only components of hacking. We will explore how hacking is used to affect society though such things as cyberwar, cyberterrorism, hacktivism and cybercrime. We will also explore the way hacking is not solely about programming or using computers when we examine connections between Creative Commons, hackers who do not programme, the programming proletariat and hacking sub-cultures. Finally, all these various components will be drawn together to consider the meaning of hacking.

All these different hacking activities exist within a set of communal relations, each of which expresses a different aspect of hacking. I stress this embeddedness in life because the hack needs a social and cultural context. The hack does not breathe well in the abstract air of philosophy or ethics but rather lives intimately entwined with a number of communities or groups of hackers. The action of the hack is thus a material practice, it occurs within various collective ethics, norms and constraints embodied in wires, code, flesh and electricity. To introduce hacking, we can look at 'the hack' and then place this action in the context of its collective material practices. Having done so we will be able then to turn back and look at hacking, hackers and the hack as a whole object, whose meaning for the twenty-first century we will then be able to examine.

Once I outline what an action has to be to have any hope of being considered a hack, I can then trace the hack in its material manifestations. This requires first examining the two key components of hacking; cracking (chapter 2) and the Free Software and Open Source movement (chapter 3). First, there are the crackers who break open your computer and sneak inside, for their own purposes. Second, there are the open so(u)rcerers who build digital freedoms through new infrastructures in the digital world. Following this we will be able to explore the complexity of hacking by adding in those who take the hack and apply it to society (chapter 4) dealing with such phenomena as war, crime, terrorism and political protest. Then we will be able to see some of the ways programming and hacking intertwine in hackers who do not programme or programmers who do not hack, as well as opening this out to see general symbolic cultures of hacking (chapter 5). Finally, the meaning of hacking can be explored allowing us to see the importance of understanding hacking for understanding the twenty-first century's obsession with information (chapter 6).

The essence of a hack

Before exploring what a hack means, two quick examples of a hack will be useful. These are not meant to capture the full picture of hacking but rather to offer specific instances.

The '@' sign used in email addresses is a hack. When the first networks were being set up email was attached to several of them as a hack; that is, programmers simply wrote means of sending mail to each other into the software controlling the network without any direction or authorisation (Quartermain 1990; Hafner and Lyon 1996: 190-2; Abatte 2000). For example, Ray Tomlinson added a means of sending electronic mail using the ARPA network, one of the most important forerunners of the Internet. He later answered the question 'Why did you do it?' by writing 'Mostly because it seemed like a neat idea. There was no directive to "go forth and invent email" . . . A colleague suggested that I not tell my boss what I had done because email wasn't in our statement of work. That was really said in jest' (Tomlinson 2006). It could have been anything, but Tomlinson chose '@' because, (1) it was a sign that did not appear in names; (2) some took '@' to mean 'at'; and (3) it was not in use on the computer systems he was thinking of (though it caused trouble for some other systems Tomlinson had forgotten about, which used '@' to mean 'erase line') (Tomlinson 2006). Another key figure in the genesis of the Internet, Jon Postel, commented when he saw Tomlinson's addition to ARPAnet, 'Now, that's a nice hack' (cited in Hafner and Lyon 1996: 192).

In June 2007, the Pentagon removed access to the Internet from as many as 1,500 computers because they had discovered a hacker had gained illicit access to an unclassified email system. It was reported that the compromised system did not contain any military information and they were taken off line to repair the security breach. Then US Secretary of Defence Robert Gates noted that Pentagon systems were subject to hundreds of hack attacks a day (Modine 2007).

Here are two very different types of hackers: Tomlinson, who acts like an engineer, and the anonymous Pentagon cracker who acts like a bandit. They both raise the question: what moves individuals to push technology beyond what it is supposed to be doing? For many, being a hacker is about autonomy, politics and fun but above all it is about making a difference in the world that presents itself to them; whether that is breaking illicitly into computers or writing the software someone wants. Torvalds described his view of hacker motivations as being beyond survival.

> A 'hacker' is a person who has gone past using his computer for survival ('I bring home the bread by programming.') . . . That is how something like Linux comes about. You don't worry about making that much money. The reason that Linux hackers do something is that they find it to be very interesting.
> (Torvalds 2001: xv)

Creativity and sharing figure large in Torvalds' interpretation of hackers' motivations. Erik Petersen – as a cracker he is a very different hacker to Torvalds – focuses in his explanation on a related but slightly different view when he was asked what it is in hacking that appeals to him: 'It's the control, the adrenaline, the knowledge, the having what you're not supposed to have' (cited in Littman 1996: 91).

The hackers Torvalds is thinking of seek something they want, something so far not implemented in a free, open operating system, and Petersen seeks hidden knowledge. The hack is the moment when a hacker gains access to these goods seemingly placed beyond him or her. The motivations are manifold; control, entertainment, adrenaline, political principles, and they all fuel the desire for access to something new, something previously unknown to the hacker.

Hackers of all sorts talk lovingly of the hack, often imbuing it with mystical properties. In a sense the hack is the way hackers touch the infinite, the way they imbue their actions with spiritual meaning and(or) change the world. This leads to an extension in which the hack has been so lovingly polished that it is at times hard to see how a hack is distinct from any creative action. Understood this way the hack need not be about computers and computer networks. Burrell Smith, an important figure in the creation of Apple's Macintosh computer argued: 'Hackers can do almost anything and be a hacker. You can be a hacker carpenter. It's not necessarily high tech. I think it has to do with craftsmanship and caring about what you're doing' (cited in Himanen 2001: 7). Put somewhat more practically, but making the same point, a hacker named Gonggrijp stated:

> it depends on how you do it, the thing is that you've got your guys that think up these things, they consider the technological elements of a phone-booth, and the they think, 'hey wait a minute, if I do this, this could work', so as an experiment, they cut the wire and it works, now THEY'RE hackers. Okay, so it's been published, so Joe Bloggs reads this and says, 'hey, great, I have to phone my folks up in Australia', so he goes out, cuts the wire, makes phone calls. He's a stupid ignoramus, yeah?
> (Cited in Taylor 1999: 18)

Gonggrijp puts his finger squarely on the point that the hack needs to create something new. Gonggrijp and Smith both point to this moment of creation noting that it can sit outside of the computer networks and computers normally associated with hackers. We reach here an abstract definition of the hack, most clearly expressed in what was *The Hacker's Dictionary* and has become *The Hacker Jargon File*, an online resource tracking the language of hackers: 'Hacking might be characterised as an "appropriate application of ingenuity"' (TJF 2006).

The writing of a programme to send electronic messages using the '@' was just such an ingenious application and while many disapprove of cracking, the Pentagon hacker obviously found an ingenious way of controlling military servers. This extension of hacking beyond the digital realm into any and all realms has been enthusiastically endorsed by some, who propound a hacker ethic as a new model for wildly divergent interests.

For example, Himanen sees hacking as a new approach to the philosophy of business. He argues that hackers represent a new 'work ethic', comparable to the Protestant work ethic that Weber argued underpinned the rise of capitalism. Himanen argues that the hacker work ethic is the spirit of the information or network society and consists of seven values: passion, freedom, social worth, openness, activity, caring and, the highest value, creativity. Himanen argues this ethic is applicable across all forms of work (Himanen 2001). In contrast, Wark sees hackers as the new revolutionary class. He argues that the information society is a third stage of property relations following from property based on land, then on capital and now on information. These stages are not successive but accumulate, each with a ruling and a revolutionary class. Hackers in their pursuit of free creativity turn out to be, for Wark, the revolutionary class of the twenty-first century (Wark 2004).

These are rather opposing views of what hacking means; from network society's handmaiden to network society's nemesis.

Wark calls himself a crypto-Marxist in opposition to Himanen's crypto-Weberianism, and accuses Himanen of aiding the ruling class by obfuscating the exploitations of network society (Wark 2004: 72 fn.). Yet despite this ideological divide, Wark and Himanen are united in defining the hack as something beyond a particular community whose primary concerns are with computers and computer networks. For Himanen, the highest and defining value of the hacker work ethic is creativity: 'creativity – that is, the imaginative use of one's own abilities, the surprising continuous surpassing of oneself and the giving to the world of a genuinely valuable contribution' (Himanen 2001: 141). For Wark:

> To hack is to differ . . . Hackers create the possibility of new things entering the world. Not always great things, or even good things, but new things. In art, in science, in philosophy and culture, in any production of knowledge where data can be gathered, where information can be extracted from it, and where in that information new possibilities for the world produced, there are hackers hacking the new out of the old.
>
> (Wark 2004: 3–4)

Both Himanen and Wark define hacking's essence as the ability to create new things, to make alterations, to produce differences. We might think of this as the abstract essence of the hack. Here we meet the nature of the hack in its plainest aspect yet we also reach a cul-de-sac, for this kind of abstraction relates to everything and nothing. The hacker R argued that 'if you haven't got a kettle to boil water with and you use your coffee machine to boil water with, then that in my mind is a hack' (cited in Taylor 1999: 16). But this is problematic, for if even the boiling of water in an unusual way is a hack then doing anything different is a hack. Any form of creativity for Himanen or any production of difference for Wark, is a hack. While finding a theoretical essence for the hack they have lost hackers and hacking. A cultural version of this freeing hacking from any relation to a specific technology or community is given by Thomas:

we must regard technology as a *cultural* and *relational* phenomenon. Doing so, I divorce the question of technology from its instrumental, technical, or scientific grounding. In fact, I will demonstrate that tools such as telephones, modems, and even computers are incidental to the actual *technology of hacking*. . . . I argue that what hackers and the discourse about hackers reveals is that technology is primarily about mediating human relationships, and that process of mediation, since the end of World War II, has grown increasingly complex. Hacking, first and foremost, is about understanding (and exploiting) those relationships.

(Thomas 2002: xx–xxi)

Again, hacking becomes everything. In Thomas' case hacking does not even refer to the specificity of innovation or the production of difference but to the mediation of human relationships. Thomas's point follows from the recognition that technologies are not asocial but, like everything else, mediated in and through social relationships. However, this should be merely a starting point; hacking will become the same as everything else if it is not developed to recognise the different relationships that produced different technologies that are characteristic of hacking. At the margins, hackers might call working on boiling water a hack but this is a margin that can only be understood from a basis in which hackers are engaged in the socially mediated technologies of computers and networked communication. For one last example, and to underline that the abstractness of a definition of hacking is not restricted to theorists such as Wark, Himanen and Thomas but is felt by hackers, here is one more hacker expanding his horizons:

In my day to day life, I find myself hacking everything imaginable. I hack traffic lights, pay phones, answering machines, micro-wave ovens, VCRs, you name it, without even thinking twice. To me hacking is just changing the conditions over and over again until there's a different response.

(Kane 1989: 67–9)

Such a view of the hack empties it of content except for such a general idea of change that the hack can become anything and everything. The objection to theories such as Wark's and Himanen's and to claims such as Kane's that I am making is that by re-interpreting a hack beyond computers and existing hacker communities, they have overgeneralised the nature of the hack and in so doing have trivialised it.

While the work we have looked at allows us to grasp something important about the hack – that it involves a moment when something new appears – we have also journeyed too far from real hackers and real hacks; we have joined in on a process of abstraction that reduces hacking to a miasma covering all social life. However, this journey has been important for two reasons. First, it allows me to distinguish this account of hacking from the overgeneralisations that permeate other accounts of hacking. Second, it means we have identified a particular moment in the creation of difference which must be present for a hack to occur. Now we need to take this creative moment and place the hack back into its social context.

The hack

At the moment we can hypothesise that the hack involves altering a pre-existing situation to produce something new; to hack is to produce differences. We can also be clear that this is too abstract and vague a description because it refers to everything, from making toast to declaring war. An understanding based on the hack as a material practice implies both the materiality of bodies and technologies in addition to the community relations that permeate and surround such bodies and technologies. To develop such a grounded definition of the hack we can take forward the examples and discussion that have already been given, but it is also important to take up existing definitions of hacking that are based on sustained empirical engagement with the hack.

Sherry Turkle argued for a particular understanding of the hack which was later endorsed by Taylor, who produced one of the first extensive empirical studies of hackers (Turkle 1984: 232; Taylor 1999: 13–15). They agreed on three characteristics of the hack.

> Simplicity: the act has to be simple but impressive
> Mastery: the act involves sophisticated technical knowledge
> Illicitness: the act is 'against the rules'.
>
> (Taylor 1999: 15)

The most important limitation of Taylor's and Turkle's definition is that it resulted from an examination of one of the subgroups of hacking: the cracking community. Accordingly, being illicit is highly valued but this is not necessarily as highly prized within the innovative cultures of free software and open source hackers. We can for the moment set aside being illicit as a core component of an all-encompassing definition of the hack, though we will come back to explore it in particular situations.

Taylor's and Turkle's work identifies an important element, which has also been implicit in the previous section. Mastery involves technical knowledge, revealing the assumption that a hack involves engagement with technology. We can take a core component of hacking to be not only producing many differences but producing these differences through engagement with some form of technology. We have seen that some wish to define this technology so widely that they produce a second version of the problem of making 'the hack' refer to everything, in that hackers such as R and Kane suggest that the hack refers to all technologies. To limit this we can note that the vast majority of hacking consists of engagement with computer, network and communications technologies. Beginning with Taylor and Turkle, we can rework the abstract, general and virtually useless definition of the hack to: a material practice that produces a difference or something new in a computer, network and/or communications technology.

Taylor and Turkle also articulated in mastery and simplicity a certain threshold of quality in a hack. It is not just the production of something new in a technology, after all pulling the plug out of a wall produces a new situation in relation to most technologies, but a hack had to demonstrate some wide technical knowledge and to be both simple and impressive. These requirements set a standard for a hack, one touched on by hacker Gonggrijp, who draws a difference between inventing a technique for making a free phone call and using that technique. The former is hacking and the latter is not. Gonggrijp then complicates this black and white example:

> The second situation is another hacker reads this and thinks 'hey, this is an idea, let's expand on this'. So what he does is go to a phone box, he cuts the wire, puts a magnetic switch in between, puts the magnetic switch up against the case, closes the door again and whenever he wants to make a free phone call, he puts a magnet on top, makes the wires disconnect, and he has a free phone call, goes away, takes the magnet away, and everybody else has to pay. Now he's more of a hacker straight away, it's not a simple black and white thing.
>
> (Cited in Taylor 1999: 18)

Stories of 'great programming hacks' often revolve around issues such as reducing the lines of software code written to successfully get a computer to conduct a particular operation, something which measures simplicity in numbers of lines. Yet, as Gonggrijp's example implies, judging what is simple and masterful is rarely as easy as counting lines of code, and further, fewer lines of code can possibly demonstrate egotism rather than technical mastery, because too compressed a form of code makes subsequent changes difficult without the original coder explaining what they have done. The latter possibility poses particular difficulties in large-scale distributed software writing projects, such as those free software and open source pursue.

Rather than attempting to define mastery and simplicity, it is more appropriate to redefine this criteria as a recognition that hacker communities will produce norms of excellence for a hack. Some crackers tend to include such things as the difficulty of the targeted system or the notoriety of the targeted system, and such considerations at times overwhelm norms related to technical mastery. Norms for hacktivists sometimes do away entirely with technical considerations and focus on poor technological solutions which better serve their political motivations. It is not possible to say across the whole of the hacking community what the particular norm for judging whether a hack is good or bad is, however it is possible to say that hackers will generate norms, even contested norms, for particular types of hack.

This points us to the final component of a definition of the hack, for the 'norms' I have just been discussing are themselves dependent on notions of community. I have already argued that notions of the hack such as those propounded by Himanen or Wark are senseless because in their hands the hack refers to everything, but a second reason why such definitions are problematic is that they are idealist. The hack becomes a free-floating form of action, disconnected from the people who hack and the material technologies that get hacked. The hack needs to be understood as that which communities both construct and reconstruct. These arguments reinforce the claim that the hack is a material practice, something that is done by people and understood and defined by collective constructions of groups of people.

A hack is, then, a material practice that produces differences in computer, network and communications technologies. The differences produced in a hack that are at stake here are twofold. First, there are differences over whether someone can control or operate their technologies. Will a website appear as the owner desires it? Or will a heading such as Central Intelligence Agency be replaced by Central Stupidity Agency? Second, there are differences produced in the nature of computer and network technologies, with hardware reworked to new ends and software written to produce new effects.

By briefly looking over the key existing work on hacking we have also uncovered two subsidiary aspects of the hack which do not at this stage appear integral but also seem closely related. Both these aspects deserve attention as we explore the nature of hacking. First, much hacking seems to utilise or desire illicit, and sometimes illegal, acts. Hacking is at times about rebellion and playing with the boundaries of what is and is not socially acceptable beyond the hacking community. Second, it is possible that hacking is more concerned than many other communities with the nature or quality of the central act that defines its community. 'Is a hack good or bad?' seems an important issue which then resolves into arguments over such things as whether a hack was derivative or original, simple or complex, technically knowledgeable or lucky.

As we explore the nature of hacking the material practice of altering technologies will form the central thread. Further, the nature of hacking as a material practice means it involves social and cultural facets. At the same time, the subsidiary aspects of being illicit and of conferring merit will be interwoven. This definition also allows me to propose a, perhaps, more accessible initial formulation of what it is that drives hackers.

The warriors of technological determinism

Technological determinism is the claim that the nature of a particular technology determines the nature of society. For example, the claim that steam energy produced industrial society or that computers create information societies. Such arguments are widely discredited because the technologies that are taken to be asocial, in that they determine society, are not asocial but are in fact socially conditioned in their invention, construction and forms of use. For some time social scientists have been able to use an accusation of 'technological determinism' as the equivalent of a disproof, almost as conclusively as pointing out that 2+2 does not equal 5.

There is no need to dispute the failure of technological determinism as an argument, as ultimately any technical system can be shown to be socially conditioned at creation and in use

(Mackenzie and Wajcman 1999). However, the success of this argument has sometimes obscured the fact that it does not address the experience of technological determinism in everyday life. The easiest way to see this is to remember moments in which a technology fails and then to review one's feelings at such moments. For example, if someone's car fails to start then they are determined by the car's technology not to be able to drive away. If a virus infects a computer and begins to make all the letters drop slowly to the bottom of the screen, then that computer's user is determined by this interaction of software and hardware not to be able to do word processing or to access email. In both these cases we could trace back the feeling of being determined by technology to demonstrate the social conditions which create petrol engines the way they are or to find the writer of the Cascade virus. To grasp the hack it is useful to recognise this day-to-day experience of being determined by technology, while simultaneously remembering that no technology is asocial.

Hackers are the warriors of this everyday technological determinism. They hack to resist being technologically determined themselves and to reform technologies so there are new determinations. If a group of hackers struggle, in their own time, to create powerful word processing software or a cleaner, faster web-browser, then they are reconstructing the forms of technological determinism within which those using such software packages will operate. If a politically motivated hacker writes a software package that hides data so that human rights activists can securely pass information, then that hacker is both contesting the ability of state-determined technologies to spy on activists and producing new technologies to serve activist politics.

Hackers are warriors of technological determinism through a dual movement. They identify where a technology is determining them in ways they dislike – from having to pay for phone calls to having email spied on – and they engage in altering that technology, which thereby automatically produces new ways in which technology can determine action. By engaging with the everyday determinations of technology, hackers enact the sociality of technology; we will constantly find hackers reconstructing the nature of a particular technology, recasting what that technology will enable a user to do, and in doing so providing living proof of the social criticism of technological determinist arguments. But, at the same time, we see that there is a constant subjection to everyday determinations of technology. The sedimented sociality of a technology – that is, the things a user can or cannot do with a technology because of all the prior social actions which produced a technology's particular nature – restricts and channels a user's possible actions in the everyday and this sense of everyday determination drives hackers to reconstruct a technology, thereby producing new levels of sedimented sociality.

Hackers are not only the warriors of technological determinism, they are most often and most importantly the warriors of determinisms deriving from computer technologies. This places them at the heart of the information or network societies that have emerged at the beginning of the twenty-first-century. Hackers open up a vital window into the possibilities, sensibilities and ethics of twenty-first-century cultures and societies. This also places them within the political, economic and cultural conflicts of these societies:

> Because of the convergence of historical evolution and technological change we have entered a purely cultural pattern of social interaction and social organization. This is why information is the key ingredient of our social organization and why flows of messages and images between networks constitute the basic thread of our social structure. . . . It is the beginning of a new existence, and indeed the beginning of a new age, the Information Age, marked by the autonomy of culture *vis-à-vis* the material bases of our existence.
>
> (Castells 2000: 508–9)

We need not go as far as Castells in proclaiming a new age for humanity to still recognise that the digital age represents significant social change and is the age of the computer and network. It is an age when information and the means of sending and receiving information are among the key structuring principles of society. We should not assume this is a new golden age, as Castells argues there are new inequalities and exploitations emerging even as old inequalities and exploitations remain or mutate into new forms. It is within the constraints and demands of twenty-first-century society that hackers operate.

Hackers are the warriors of the information society because they constantly grapple with the everyday determinations of information technologies. Hackers lead us to the heart of the twenty-first century and the digital cultures that make up the information age.

CHAPTER TWO

Cracking: Black Hats on the Internet

SQL Injection: whose computer?

Someone sitting at a computer connected to the Internet has an everyday moment in which the site they try to connect to asks for a username and password. Normally this will be something recognisable like TimJordan or TimJ as a username and a password initially given to TimJ but most likely then changed by him to something he is likely to remember (memory being an issue for many of us given the number of passwords that accumulate). This user, who is not TimJ, instead entered the following for username and then exactly the same string of characters for the password:

'or where password like – %'

This user had no legitimate account on the targeted computer and his purpose in going to this site was to try and steal a list of people who use the site, because he had been asked to supply lists of people with tastes catered for by such sites (in this case, a taste for bondage pornography but it might have as easily been science fiction) (Mitnick and Simon 2005: 166–77). By breaking into websites which already service a particular interest, this computer user can hopefully obtain email lists that identify a ready-made market for his employer.

The point of entering that particular string of characters for username and password is that the computer that receives the command reads it in a particular way, which offers unexpected results. In this case, a database of legitimate usernames and passwords is being queried in the hope of an illegitimate user gaining entry to the site. The command that has been entered is read by the database as: select a record from the database of users where the username is like ' ' or is like % and the password is like ' ' or is like %. But % is a wild card, it tells the computer to return the record if the username or password is anything at all (the ' ' is included to make the command readable to the computer). Having been instructed in legitimate SQL language, even if by someone illegitimate, to allow a user access with any username and any password, the computer agrees and logs this person into the first account in its database. As it is common for the administrator – that is, the person who controls, alters and manages the website and database – to be listed first in the database, our illicit user will most likely be logged in as the administrator and will have all he or she needs to control the targeted site (Mitnick and Simon 2005: 175).

This true story is about a hack more often now called a crack. The targeted computer was cracked open due to a combination of insecure implementation of SQL and the intruder's knowledge of SQL vulnerabilities. In this attack a computer thought to be controlled by one person became simultaneously the plaything of another. Crackers have been for many years the spectacular public face of hacking; there was the hacker who peeked into the husband of the Queen of England's electronic mailbox (the password was 1234); the hacker who, in search of information about UFOs, broke into and explored hundreds of US military sites; the hacker who controlled telephones constantly cutting someone off; the hacker who argued with a civil rights activist and made his point by posting the activist's credit records into the debate; and, the hacker who was supposed to be able to fire nuclear weapons by whistling down a phone. Only the last of these is untrue, though it was used as a reason to prevent one hacker (Kevin Mitnick) from using a phone while he was in custody.

In the early 1990s, crackers gained such extensive media attention that hacking began to mean illicit computer intrusion and all other meanings of the term hacking began to dis-appear from public discussion. Yet cracking embodies only one side of hacking and, for many, it is hacking's dark side, where expertise employed to produce a hack is also employed to dominate other people's technology – taunting and dismiss-ing anyone who can be cracked. By looking at cracking first, I run the risk of reinforcing the media fuelled mistake of equat-ing cracking with hacking, but at the same time I can focus immediately on what is most likely to be best known about hacking.

Cracks in electronic walls

The starting point is, then, that a crack is a distinct type of hack. I have argued that hacking is a material practice that alters technologies, which may or may not have illicit and meritocratic aspects. Further, these material practices will be aimed centrally at various everyday determinations created by technologies, which the hack/crack will seek to subvert, put-ting into effect a new form of determination. In the case of SQL injection attacks, we see a particular technologically determining moment – I must enter my username and pass-word to gain access – subverted through an unexpected use of SQL commands, allowing a new situation to emerge – the cracker gained full access and control allowing them to steal a database of subscribers. We can build on this definition of the hack and identify four types of cracks that are prevalent. Outlining each briefly with an example will allow a clear view of the nature of the hack that cracks. The four types are zero-day exploits, zero-plus-one-day exploits, social engineering and script-kidding. Each of these represents a type of crack that breaks down the electronic walls that secure data on, and control over, any computer.

Zero-day exploits refer to the very first time a vulnerability is used to crack a computer or network open. Once the exploit has been used, every day after is one on which the vulnerable software or hardware could be fixed (Mitnick and Simon 2005: 45). An example is one of the most famous hacks of all, one of the few ever turned into a movie as well as at least three different books, with the hacker's (assumed by most to be Kevin Mitnick) own account still to be published.[1] This was the cracking open of security analyst Tsuotumo Shimomura's computer with an IP-spoofing attack. The target, Shimomura, pointed out that 'This was an "IP-spoofing" attack, a type that had been described in theory in the computer science literature but which, as far as I knew, had never before been carried out as a hostile attack' (Shimomura 1995: 91). Shimomura's subsequent use of this attack in lectures to demonstrate the reality of this vulnerability to other computer security professionals underlines the fact it was a recorded zero-day attack.

The target was Shimomura's personal computer network, consisting of a series of computers some of which 'trusted' each other – that is, they allowed data traffic to pass freely between them and commands to be executed but were also secured from the wider Internet and other computers. The cracker first attacked by sending a series of commands across the Internet from a cracked computer located on the West Coast of the USA, which elicited information that allowed a map of Shimomura's network to be drawn. Once two computers that trusted each other had been identified (named by Shimomura as Osiris and Rimmon), the cracker began sending a rapid series of requests to connect to Rimmon from another cracked computer in Switzerland. Then, three seconds after Rimmon was tied up with a flood of requests, a series of requests to connect were made to Osiris from a third cracked computer based at a Chicago university. This series of requests was a means of testing what Osiris expected to hear from Rimmon when the two communicated; with Rimmon effectively gagged by the flood of requests to it from the Swiss-based computer, the Chicago-based attack could probe Osiris until it could pretend to be Rimmon and suddenly the attacker would find themselves inside Osiris. Shimomura describes this process as like the technique employed by some shops to manage queues by giving a ticket with a number to customers, who are then served in numbered order. The cracker was able to work out which number Rimmon would use to request service and so was able to get Osiris to serve them (Shimomura 1995: 86–91). From this point on, Shimomura's computers were cracked open and the first command issued by the cracker was 'echo + + >/.rhosts' which told Osiris to drop any defence and allow anyone to connect without a password (Shimomura 1995: 90).

A zero-day attack exhibits two aspects. First, there is the identification of some kind of vulnerability, and in this case it was identified as a possibility in 1984, eleven years before this particular attack, and was fully outlined in a 1989 paper (Shimomura 1995: 91; Tanase 2003). The second aspect is the theory being put into practice, which we have followed through in this example. Zero-day attacks are by definition innovative, either or both in theory and practice, because they have not been achieved before.

Zero-plus-one-day exploits use an existing attack. For example, someone utilising an IP-spoofing attack who had read about the Shimomura crack and then researched how to conduct one, perhaps using resources such as daemon9/route/infinity's guide in hacker journal Phrack (daemon9/route/infinity 1996), would be using a zero-plus-one-day attack. These attacks are not innovative in a fundamental sense but demonstrate lesser or more complexity depending on the target. For example, it is well known that software engineers often do not change default passwords and that the range of possible defaults is well known (for example, a common one is: username: admin; password: admin). A known and simple hack is simply to try possible passwords. For example, the cracker who obtained access to the Duke of Edinburgh's mailbox accidentally found a username (by randomly typing '2' ten times) and then, he recounted, 'I hit the 2 button, ten times and it said "yeah, fine what's the password?", so I thought "this is easy, I know passwords are four characters so I'll try 1234", tried 1234 and it let me in and it turned out to be an internal BT [British Telecom] account that let me access loads of closed areas on the system' (Schifreen cited in Taylor 1999: 72).

Testing targeted systems for well-known vulnerabilities, such as not changing default passwords or not protecting against IP-spoofing, is the bread and butter of zero-plus-one-day attacks. The SQL injection attack that this chapter began with is another such attack. The new determinations of technology, the hacks, are here less the knowledge of vulnerabilities than creative uses of existing techniques. For example, though SQL injection attacks are known they may take different forms. Rather than the demented elegance of telling a system to log someone on if they have any username and any password, different uses of SQL might be found. Another account of an SQL attack culminates in the following command being issued from the attacker to the targeted system:

> SELECT email, passwd, login_id, full_name
> FROM members
> WHERE email = 'x';
> UPDATE members
> SET email = 'steve@unixwiz.net'
> WHERE email = 'bob@example.com';

(Friedel 2005)

The attacker here has first probed this system to identify how SQL is set up and what vulnerabilities there are. They had noted that the system employed a common facility to request a new password be sent to an email address already registered in the database. They also found they were allowed to execute commands. This is shown in the line 'WHERE email = "x"; Update . . .' in which everything after the semi-colon can be a SQL command which will be executed. The attacker had also turned up a legitimate email address registered on this system, here represented as the fake address 'bob@example.com'. Executing the command quoted above means that the database was ordered to

update itself replacing 'bob@example.com' with 'steve@
unixwiz.net'. Once this was done, it was a simple matter to click
on the request for a new password and it was sent to Steve's
email address rather than Bob's, giving Steve a legitimate username and password.

It might seem obvious to have zero and zero-plus attacks,
one implies the other, yet it is worth distinguishing them
because zero-plus attacks are not the simple recipe reading that
they might seem. Rather, as we see in the account of
steve@example.com's crack, after doing some probing he was
able to add together the three elements of a valid email address,
the ability to execute SQL code and the ability to request a password to a valid email account and come up with another version
of an SQL attack. Zero-plus-one-day attacks range from the
simplistic to the complex but all involve knowledge of existing
attacks and vulnerabilities. They work to turn technological
determinations inside out, with the added spice that the determinations being explored are known but the cracker cannot be
sure what they will find on any particular system.

The zero and zero-plus attacks are primarily about
research – either of unconfirmed vulnerabilities or of the vulnerabilities of a specific system – and then having the technical skills to execute a theory. The cracks in the electronic walls
are technological and are attacked or created with interventions into technologies. The third type of crack seeks to exploit
the fact that technological systems interact constantly with
humans. Social engineering is the term for techniques that
seek to crack open a system by tricking a human into giving
out information. The logic is, why go to the trouble of an SQL
attack, when you can phone someone up, pretend to be a software engineer seeking to solve a critical problem and have
someone on the end of the phone line give you a valid username and password? There are a range of such social engineering attacks, such as shoulder surfing, which involves
looking over someone's shoulder and memorising details as
they type, or impersonating technical staff, where the cracker

uses their technical knowledge to convince an employee of a company that the cracker is also an employee. All such attacks involve some kind of personal subterfuge to open up a crack in the walls (Mitnick and Simon 2005).

For example, in 2003, a small survey was done in London's Waterloo train station. Commuters were offered a cheap pen if they were willing to give over their work computer password and 95 per cent of men and 85 per cent of women were willing to do so. One male who refused to provide his password did mention during the conversation that the password was his daughter's name. He was asked what his daughter's name was and happily supplied it. No particular technical expertise was on show here, just a reminder of how easy it can be to persuade people to give up the information that secures their computer (Leyden 2003).

We see here how social engineering substitutes for the previous two types of attacks, which rely on knowledge of technological norms, an attack based on knowledge of social norms. This raises the issue of whether social engineering is a hack at all because the access to technology is achieved without technology. However, to suggest this is to miss the fact that the material practices that produce a change in technological determination need not themselves be technologically focused. Rather, social engineering focuses on social material practices – such as trusting those with obvious technical know-how, or assuming anyone in a secure area is there legitimately simply because they are already there – that can be exploited for entry to technological systems. This underlines the fact that we should never distinguish technology from society if by that we mean technologies should be designated as asocial. Social engineering cracks alter technologies by illicitly opening them up to access but do so by identifying predominantly social practices that are vulnerable rather than focusing on predominantly technological practices.

The final category of crackers are often dismissively called script-kiddies. Freedman's and Mann's account of one of the

most persistent, successful but often least adept hackers captures the spirit of a script-kiddy. In this account Phantomd is
the persistent cracker and Grok is a more experienced and
skilled cracker.

> Many of the #hackers gave Phantomd a hard time. They
> called him a wannabe, a lamer, a poser. They said he was
> stupid. Grok, by contrast, treated Phantomd as a youthful
> version of himself, an aspiring colleague, an open vessel in
> which to decant knowledge. He provided Phantomd with
> some programs – fifteen minutes' work for Grok, but a life-
> changing event of importance for Phantomd. . . . Without
> them Phantomd was no more than the lamer derided by the
> crew at #hack. Tools in hand, he was the functional equivalent
> of Grok. His lack of knowledge didn't matter; if he pushed the
> right buttons, the programs would do all the work for him.
>   (Freedman and Mann 1997: 62)

Pushing buttons on programmes that embody someone else's
knowledge rather than typing out commands based on a
cracker's own knowledge is the essence of scripting. This
replacement of expertise with button pushing (the replacement of the cracker's expertise with someone else's expertise
that has been embodied in a programme) is the reason why the
term 'script-kiddy' is considered an insult within hacking; it
carries the ultimate taint of not only having no skills but covering this up by using other people's skills through the scripts
contained in programmes.

An example is the programme stacheldraht,[2] written origi-
nally by a hacker called the Mixter. This programme automates
the launching of a distributed denial of service attack (DDOS).
Such attacks focus on removing a targeted site from the
Internet by sending so many packets of information to the
target so quickly that the targeted site simply cannot handle
the flow and is effectively gagged and bound, making it seem to
all others on the Internet as if the site has disappeared. This is
achieved in two stages. First, the attacker places a programme
on as many cracked computers connected to the Internet as the

cracker can exploit. Second, all the programmes on the cracked computers must be told when and where to send data when an attack is initiated. Stacheldraht co-ordinates this process, allowing an attacker to order what can be thousands of other computers across the Internet to simultaneously start sending data packets to a target, the effect of which can be devastating (Dittrich 1999). Such well-funded, defended and established sites as amazon.com, ebay.com and cnn.com have been suddenly eliminated from the Internet using such methods, though it is not clear that these particular attacks used stacheldraht. For example, an attack on ebay.com used 20,000 computers to generate data (Sooman 2005).

The hack in this form of crack is the writing of the programme, whereas its use is considered by many hackers to be an unoriginal over-reliance on others' expertise. Here the technological determinations and their remaking are twofold. First, the writers of programmes create another piece of technology which allows and disallows certain actions. This writing is itself innovative, and there may be different programs for the same kind of attack (for example, for DDOS there are at least three: trinoo, stacheldraht and Tribal Floodnet). Second, there is the use of such programmes which in themselves often have only passing, if traumatic, effects.

Each of the four types of cracks I have outlined is a material practice, it must be enacted in relation to various repeated interactions between objects and humans. Each crack opens up a technological moment in which access to or control over some computer systems pass from one entity to the cracker, even though the initial entity does not wish this transfer to happen. If we remember that hacks are material practices which produce differences in computer and network technologies, then cracks are the hacks which devote themselves to illicitly transferring control over computers and networks. Cracks, in a sense, produce nothing new in the infrastructures of virtuality, rather they are passing moments; for example, a defaced website can often be returned to its normal state with a few copied files. It is only in collective responses to hacks that the infrastructure of virtuality is affected by cracking.

There are two limit cases within these archetypes of cracking. Social engineering points out that transferring control over a computer system can be done by cracking social norms rather than technical norms. Social engineering is a crack, it involves tactics which produce illicit access to or control over a computer system, but it is at the limit of a hack as its material practices bracket out much technology and its essence is in social and cultural manipulation. The second limit case is the use of scripts, which is also clearly a crack but is at one degree removed; it is a crack done through someone else's hack. Unlike social engineering, this is clearly inside the technical frame of hacking but suggests a different limit to the hack in the potential for rote use of scripts instead of ingenuity. Hacks are, in a sense, first-order acts whereas script-kiddy style actions operate at a second order.

While we have clarified how hacks and cracks are closely related we have reached a small paradox in that some of the core activities of cracking are clearly hacks and some seem either to not be hacks or to push at the boundaries of hacking. Yet all such actions clearly relate to, and are often central to, cracking. We have reached this state by focusing on, and thereby isolating somewhat illegitimately, the act of the crack from the crackers and their social, cultural and technological relations – I have allowed the crack to become isolated from the cracking and hacking community. To complete the picture of crackers, we now need to turn back to the cracking community and give zero-day, zero-plus-one-day, social engineering and script-kiddy cracks a fuller context and meaning.

Cracking communities

In exploring hacking I have moved from seemingly separate, even individual, moments in which a hack or crack occurs to a characterisation of these actions as some form of common material practice. This leads to the reflection that a material, collective, practice makes sense only within various social or cultural contexts. Such contexts have also, so far, commonly been called communities. The cracking community is the general context of social and cultural practices which surround, support and enable the particular practice of the crack.

A number of characterisations of the cracking community exist in other studies. Among academic analyses three are notable. First, Taylor's, which is based on one of the few extensive empirical studies, lists the characteristics of cracking to be: technology content, secrecy and fluidity, youth and generation gap, gender and misogyny, anonymity and motivations (Taylor 1999: 37–65). In relation to this groundbreaking work, Taylor and I refined his categories arguing that the internal dynamics of the cracking community were constituted out of six different norms; technology, secrecy, anonymity, membership fluidity, male dominance and motivations (Jordan and Taylor 1998). Thomas argues crackers (and hackers) engage constantly with secrecy from the basis of being a 'boy culture' whose constitutive traits are confrontation with adult authority, mastery over technology and independence (Thomas 2002: x). Clearly these three efforts, two of which derive from Taylor's data, reflect similarities. Cracking has also attracted considerable journalistic research which usually focuses on telling a particular story of a crack or crackers rather than filling in complexities of community structure. However, Sterling's seminal account of the police crackdown on US hacking in the late 1980s and early 1990s suggests the following are key aspects of cracking: access to forbidden knowledge; use of language; fast turnover of members; small numbers but strongly interconnected communication; peer education; low-level and limited forms of formal organisation; and, a desire for exploration (Sterling 1992: 58–92). Many factors noted by Sterling cross over and reflect those in academic studies and are often repeated in studies about, and stories of, crackers that do not provide an overall analysis of cracking.

These overviews of community suggest a number of
common traits, including: secrecy, masculinity, confrontation
and technology. Hardly unique to cracking cultures, such traits
might well fit several different communities. The specificity of
cracking emerges more clearly if we consider the underlying
dynamics which produces such common traits among crackers, and also allows us to identify the particular form of secrecy
or adventure that concerns crackers. There are two key social
processes which centrally define the cracking community:
peer recognition and peer education. There are also a number
of other processes which revolve around and complicate the
central dynamic set up by peer recognition and education –
which I believe are best understood as symbols, secrecy, confrontation and masculinity. These social processes are most
easily described if we treat them as being internal to the cracking community, as processes operating between crackers, but
they are in reality constantly battered by processes which
engage crackers with non-crackers. Having outlined in a limited fashion the central dynamic, it will then be important to
outline how the internal and external processes relevant to a
cracking community interact. This should be stressed, for the
presentation of the structures of the cracking community
abstracts from the messy reality of crackers, the media, computer security experts and sundry others interacting.

Peer recognition names the processes by which crackers
both refer to each other as crackers and judge each other's
merit as crackers. Such processes are common in any community, what is key is the centrality of this process for crackers
who mainly and habitually communicate with each other in a
disembodied, text-based environment about fast-changing
technologies. In such a context, peer recognition derives from
knowledge about such technologies and from evidence of
having successfully utilised such knowledge. The latter
explains the rather paradoxical habit crackers have of taking
trophies, that is, of copying some kind of information that
could only be gained from a cracked computer. This is

paradoxical, as such trophies, as is well known among crackers, provide some of the only solid evidence many prosecutors
can use in court cases. However, such trophy taking is itself
beset by difficulties as it is easy enough to copy such trophies
once shown one by someone else. This problem of the ease
of duplicating digital trophies as a means of generating peer
recognition leads to the alternative of demonstrating the
knowledge that allowed the trophy to be taken, and thus immediately integrates peer education because demonstrating that
one knows something is, among crackers, the equivalent to
teaching it. This is because the process of a cracker proving
they have knowledge involves them teaching that knowledge to
someone else who then verifies the knowledge by doing what
they have just been taught. Any cracker who claims to know
how to exploit a particular fault in a computer will be quickly
tested by other crackers demanding to know how to do the
exploit and then going off to test whether it works or not. Any
cracker who refuses to teach their exploit, and so to prove the
exploit really works, will usually be considered a fake.

Peer recognition, both in terms of acceptance as a cracker
and in proving how good or bad a cracker someone is, and peer
education, which functions both to pass on skills and to legitimate claims to peer recognition, are closely intertwined as the
central social dynamic of crackers. This can be seen in the following episode involving two crackers. Phantomd was a
cracker often considered by his peers as poorly skilled and
mocked by other crackers; and Grok, who was widely considered an elegant and knowledgeable cracker. This retelling of
the incident is by authors Freedman and Mann and it begins
with Grok having lost access to the Internet and considering
how to get it back:

> Which seems to have led him [Grok] to recall the greenhorn
> Phantomd. . . . Any network that would let somebody like
> him run around freely was worth enquiring into.
>   Grok broke into Portland State and created an account with
> an inconspicuous name. As he had suspected Phantomd had

stumbled across the perfect network: a system with full Internet connectivity whose sysadmins . . . were touchingly naïve about security. . . . They hadn't realized that he [Phantomd] had created half a dozen accounts for himself and was brazenly copying their e-mail . . . Kind of funny, watching an utter amateur nail the pros.

Then Grok got nailed, too. He was changing his account name – a precaution to avoid having too much activity associated with a single user – when Phantomd unexpectedly asked the Portland State machine what programs were running. Discovering the name changing program, Phantomd correctly reasoned that because ordinary users had little reason to change their account names, the other person must be a cracker. To his mortification, Grok received a cheerful message: Hey, there! I see you!

(Freedman and Mann 1997: 57)

The cheerful message will have popped as text onto Grok's screen, marking a moment in which the previously unrespected Phantomd reorders recognition between the two crackers. Phantomd forced peer recognition through the undeniable cracker ability of both illicitly entering a system but also monitoring that system and identifying different behaviour. Grok was unlikely to quickly abandon his low opinion of Phantomd but he was also caught, unable to deny some recognition to Phantomd. The account continues.

> Grok ignored him.
> 'Who are you?' Phantomd asked.
> No response.
> 'I see you', Phantomd wrote. 'You can't hide from me'.
> Grok gave up. The novice had whacked another expert. Now Grok could either acknowledge the call or log off the network. Logging off would be too humiliating. 'Make a sign', he wrote.
> It was an elite way, Phantomd knew, of saying: 'Speak to me'.
> 'Who is this?' Phantomd wanted to know. 'What are you doing? What are you up to?'
> The chagrined Grok told the truth.

> Phantomd was overjoyed. At last he had the attention of
> the celebrated Grok! Grok, caught, launched what was in
> effect a tutorial. Although sometimes slow to pick things up,
> Phantomd proved an eager student.
>
> (Freedman and Mann 1997: 57–8)

Grok responded to being caught initially in a way that only someone already familiar with elite hacking would recognise – typing 'Speak to me' and sending it. Phantomd, never previously allowed by other elite hackers even minimal respect, was now being offered a kind of 'hello' which, like a mason's secret handshake, offered recognition and the beginnings of acceptance into the elite. And immediately this recognition was offered, there followed education. Grok explained what he was doing in such a way as to educate Phantomd. This education was made explicit as Grok allowed Phantomd to ask questions and to have things repeated until he grasped them.

This exchange, even though it was reported to us by journalists, whose accuracy concerning hackers and crackers is not always to be trusted, exemplifies the close and dynamic interrelation between peer recognition and peer education. Recognition can usually only be expressed in ways that automatically allow education, in this way harnessing the desire for status to the drive to learn. Such a dynamic partly explains the constantly rising technical efficiency of cracking attacks and the openness with which crackers, even those who see themselves as being in competition, share information and techniques.

We also see in the Grok–Phantomd moment some of the other key factors which flow around the central dynamic of status and learning. Like nearly all cultures and sub-cultures, crackers develop their own symbols, in this case the 'Speak to me' has a significance which all but another cracker would most likely miss. Secrecy is also present, as though Grok is already known to Phantomd, Phantomd cannot know it is Grok in this particular instance because Grok appears to Phantomd merely as some username who is running a programme that implies this person is a cracker. Confrontation is readily present as seen both in the confrontation implied by two crackers who invade someone else's network and in Phantomd's immediate confrontation of Grok. What is implicit in this anecdote is the masculinity which dominates cracking cultures. It will be useful to outline briefly each of these elements of cracking communities in turn.

Symbols, secrecy, confrontation, masculinity

Looking at the symbols crackers use reinforces the textual nature of this culture. Most communication between crackers is carried over the Internet using text-based chat systems such as IRC. The typical ways of interacting which identify crackers to each other develop mainly in typed text. The obvious example is the emergence of 'leet' speak, a seriously strange dialect of English which has been heavily influenced by cracking, but also by gaming communities. Leet speak has its own neologisms and conventions. For example, numbers may be used to replace letters; leet being spelt l33t. Or ironic references to the origins of communication in fingers running across keyboards are used, as can be seen in the way 1 comes to stand for an exclamation mark, something that can easily happen if the shift key is missed. Just as Grok could use a short phrase 'Speak to me', so many crackers have shorthand and jargon they can use both to claim their own status as crackers and to signal to other crackers. This kind of textual communication also distances crackers from each other, removing all cues of looks, voice texture and expression. This has been somewhat ameliorated by increasing use of various forms of voice over the Internet (voip) but it remains constituent to cracking cultures that identities are mediated by text rather than body.

Cracking has an ambivalent attitude to secrecy and anonymity, which is best exemplified in its attitude to naming. Crackers usually hide behind various online names or handles, as we have seen with Grok and Phantomd (whose real name was Matt Singer). This allows an ongoing identity to be constructed by a cracker as a good or bad cracker but at the same time masks their real world identity. This ambivalence is driven by the illicit nature of cracking, requiring attention to be paid to the possibility of arrest and prosecution, while at the same time there is a need to participate in peer recognition. A similar ambivalence is manifested, as already noted, in crackers' habits of taking trophies from sites they have broken into, thereby often storing the best evidence of their crimes on their own computers. Secrecy and anonymity are simultaneously denied and desired.

Crackers also have a taste for confrontation in their constant desire to break into systems that want to keep them out, simply to prove they can do it and to use this to build peer recognition. Crackers have been known to contact the administrators of sites they have broken into in order to tell the administrator to improve their security. Crackers organise conferences; as police have wryly pointed out they are the only criminal society to hold open, publicly advertised conferences at which they discuss their criminality. Confrontation, both the willingness to undertake it and the admiration gained from it, is another cultural link between crackers. This works in a contradictory fashion in relation to secrecy because confrontation attracts attention but also demands anonymity to defuse consequences. At times confrontation over-rides secrecy, as when the cracking community makes itself public, with hackers speaking at conferences or reacting to news events by talking to the media. At other times, confrontation relies on the ambivalence of cracking and secrecy when crackers confront major systems and seek to break into them, knowing publicity and pursuit are likely to follow.

Crackers have a culture constituted out of symbolic resources based on textual creativity, reliant on an ambivalent addiction to secrecy and fatally attracted to confrontation. Threaded through these three elements of cracker culture is the simple demographic fact that the vast majority of crackers have been male. This means an un-thought masculinity runs through cracking, ranging from a separate spheres notion that hacking reflects the natural world in which women are interested in birthing and building whereas men are interested in exploring and conquering, to a misogynistic streak which pursues and persecutes women. The hacker Freiss notes that the perception of being anonymous online leads many men to drop civilised habits, leading to harassment of women by email being 'not uncommon'. Another hacker, Mercury, argued that 'my wife programs and she has the skills of a hacker. She has had to crack security in order to do her job. But she does it as her job, not for the abstract thrill of discovering the unknown. . . . Females who compute would rather spend their time building a good system, than breaking into someone else's system' (cited in Jordan and Taylor 1998: 767–8).

The community of cracking is driven by a mechanism that integrates peer recognition and peer education as its motor and around which flow cultures of text-based symbols, ambivalence towards secrecy, desire for confrontation and masculine norms. While this description encompasses the key elements of cracking, it has so far isolated cracking from time and space, failing to locate historical or geographical trends. To conclude, we can take this overview of cracks and put them back into the world they occurred in.

Cracking in time and space

Cracking can be, roughly, divided into three spaces and three phases in time which interact with each other. Geographically, cracking tends to follow increasing access to computer networks, meaning that the space of cracking is disjointed, with the USA being key in the initial phase when phone phreaking (the term for illicit use of telephones) turned into computer cracking. As the use of computers expanded and computer networks of various sorts emerged, the second phase emerged, which we can call the golden era of cracking, in which the USA is key but those of Europe and some specific sites in Eastern Europe are also important. Finally, the current state of cracking emerges with the success of police crackdowns and the spread of computer networks worldwide, particularly the Internet, meaning that cracking communities emerge in all connected spaces. In this division of cracking, phases in time suggest changes in which the old is surpassed by the new, but changes in space suggest accumulation in which the old persists alongside the new (for example, the USA remains important all through the history of cracking). Throughout these changes in space and time different communities outside crackers shift in and out of focus, becoming more and less important as cracking shifts in nature.

Phone phreaking refers to the various means of cracking phone systems both to gain free phone calls and to be able to play with the phone system. Techniques were as simple as whistling down a phone (on some phone systems the correct tone unlocked abilities) to full-blown cracks of software running more advanced phone systems. In the late 1960s phone phreaking was drawn into US counter-cultures and became, for a short time, associated particularly with the Yippies (Thomas 2002: 16). As these counter-cultures waned in the 1970s, phone phreaking gradually became totally concerned with the technical aspects of invading phone systems. Such activity in the late 1960s and into the mid 1970s can be found in nearly any space in which pay phone calls operated. This tended to be a fragmented space, the key to which was the lack of a widely accessible many-to-many form of communication, which inhibited development beyond local links between phreakers. As phone systems began to make greater use of computers, so phreaking began to develop cracking tendencies.

At the same time as phone systems were becoming more dependent on computers, so computers were emerging in schools and universities. As personal computers also emerged in the late 1970s (the Altair 8800 is widely considered the earliest personal computer and it was first produced in 1975) more individuals were gaining programming skills and knowledge of how to manipulate computers. Finally, a third current was simultaneously gathering speed with the emergence of computer networks. Though mainly government funded university-based networks, these were gradually gaining in significance. Such networks would begin, in the 1980s, to develop more grassroots versions using modems and personal-computer-hosted bulletin boards leading to networks such as Fidonet. These latter systems were developed and supported particularly in the USA, leading to a significant impact by US crackers.

The culmination of these three trends was that cracking solidified as a clear form of action and community. Phreaking was developing significant computer expertise in assaults on phone networks, while more people were gaining computer expertise and access to computer networks was expanding. Though still usually focused on phone systems and also still spatially fragmented, the first phase of cracking passed as the three trends lead to the golden age of cracking (Thomas 2004).

The golden age of cracking stretched from the early to mid 1980s until the late 1990s. It is marked at its beginning by increasing use of bulletin boards and the Internet to construct communications between cracker groups, producing an increase in the speed at which cracking innovations are made, and it is marked at its end by increasing criminalisation, crackdowns and a shift into ever-greyer areas of activity. The identities of US-based crackers solidifies in the early stages of 'the golden age', while at the same time contrasting European (largely UK, German and Dutch) identities were formed. This produces some of the clearest spatial divisions between crackers, who habitually see space as smooth, stretching out evenly into ageographic information networks. A number of other cracking geographies emerged during this period, most notably when Bulgarian university teaching seemed to produce a core of virus writers (see chapter 5) and when a small number of Australian crackers produced a notable politicised assault on Nasa.

As Internet access emerges more and more widely during this period, and networks such as Fidonet produce other pre-Internet forms of networked information, crackers move away from a focus on phone services. By the mid-1990s phones remain an interest, but now the focus is more on understanding and manipulating systems across the Internet. As access to the Internet becomes easier, the need to manipulate phone systems for free phone calls diminishes and so does the desire to crack phone systems. American crackers solidify an identity through social resources such as the emergence of conferences and journals like Phrack and 2600 and through a confrontation with law enforcement which, belatedly recognising the potentially serious nature of computer crime, begins to form dedicated counter-groups and to conduct specific crackdowns. European crackers also form some notable resources, such as XS4ALL and the Chaos Computer Club, but develop a distinct identity to US-based crackers, though often this identity relates more to rhetorical resources – particularly a fondness for anarchist rhetoric against US-based crackers' fondness for libertarian ideas – than it does to distinct cracking techniques (Hafner and Markoff 1991). Simultaneously, cracking gains significant media attention, with the increasing importance of computer networks becoming obvious to all, and the notion of crackers who can interfere with such networks becoming threatening and newsworthy. It is in this period that the mass media's repetition of the term 'hacker' when reporting the exploits of crackers leads to hacker becoming, outside of expert computer communities, the term most people use to describe crackers.

With computer security low on many people's agendas, particularly large institutions which have developed computer networks and Internet access often without understanding their significance, with the police always seemingly several steps behind and with an information landscape in the Internet that is expanding at an astounding speed, this period can in many ways be described justly as golden for crackers (Thomas 2004). Geographically, the division that seems to initially emerge between USA and European crackers, and for a while seemed to be being replicated with Australian then Israeli and other groups claiming distinct identities, actually begins to diminish as the ability to communicate swiftly around the globe begins to create a sense that cracking unites more than geographically based cultures divide.

The golden age begins to fall apart under a number of pressures. The chief pressure is the increasing criminalisation of cracking, with a series of laws passed by nation-states to outlaw cracking, and law enforcement becoming ever more committed to catching and jailing crackers. While not preventing cracking, or even gaining a commensurate level of expertise relating to crackers, police and security agencies undermine the sense of immunity from capture and prosecution that many seemed to feel in the golden age. Increasing access to the Internet also undermines a key reason why crackers who were fascinated by the Internet engaged in cracking; they no longer had any need to generate access illicitly.

The final phase of cracking comes out of these changes, with cracking continuing to this day. For example, in 2002 Gary McKinnon was accused of cracking a long series of US military computer sites while searching for evidence of UFO cover-ups by the US military. He was extradited to the USA in 2006, even though UK authorities had declined to prosecute him. McKinnon's exploits reflect ongoing cracks against even highly secured targets but also underlines that state prosecution is ever present (see chapter 4). The complexity of cracks continues to grow and the dynamics of peer recognition and peer education remain powerful. However, the increasing importance of the Internet means both that police and security agencies pay ever more attention to cracking but also that cracking with criminal intent offers ever greater rewards. This is leading to a rift within the cracking community, as

some cracking shifts ever further toward criminal enter-
prises, including organised crime, while some crackers retain
their identity as explorers of the virtual world who disdain
financial profit. It is impossible at the time of writing to fore-
tell the future of cracking. However, it is also clear that the
trend is toward, on the one hand, the ongoing maintenance of
cracking and its community as it has been described in this
chapter and, on the other hand, the emergence of large-scale
criminal cracking.

Concluding cracking

Crackers engage closely with technological determinations of
society and social determinations of technology in computer
and network technologies, breaking them down into techniques and adventures that constantly alter the nature of the
Internet. Yet, cracks are also, in a sense, ephemeral. The effects
of a crack can often be quickly erased; a website can be restored
to its original state simply by copying files, a site removed by a
DDOS attack will often reappear within hours. Crackers strike
and then drift away, back to their chat rooms to discuss what
they have done.

This ghost-like quality to the effects of cracking results from
cracking's individualistic nature. Not that crackers act alone, as
most crackers are in communication with other crackers, but
that their acts are momentary and are capable of being taken by
an individual. The interventions of crackers, as devastating as
they can be, also pass by in the great wash of information flowing around the Internet.

Cracking embeds within hacking a desire to constantly test
and deconstruct technologies, both uncovering embedded
social determinations and altering them. Crackers extend into
individual control over computer hacking's ability to simultaneously combine social determinations of technologies and
technological determinations of social moments. Crackers are
the transgressors of hacking.

Notes

1 In 2005 Mitnick referred in his acknowledgements to 'In a little over two years, I'll finally be able to write and publish The Untold Story of Kevin Mitnick, after certain government restrictions expire' (Mitnick and Simon 2005: xi).

2 *Stacheldraht* means 'barbed wire' in German.

CHAPTER THREE

Free Software and Open Source: Collaboration, Objects and Property

Introduction: the meaning of software

One of the most famous statements in hacking's history came in what was called 'A Letter To Hobbyists'. The letter was written in 1976 by a nineteen-year-old who ran a small software company and it was prompted by the copying without payment of some of the software his company had written. After noting that there appeared to be many more copies of his programme in use than he had been paid for and that the labour his company put into this particular programme now worked out at less than $2 per hour, the budding entrepreneur drew the conclusion that most computer hobbyists were stealing his company's software. After accusing computer hobbyists of theft, the letter writer added a second argument by claiming that such robbery would in the long run hurt the very people who were stealing his software.

> One thing you do do is prevent good software from being written. Who can afford to do professional work for nothing? What hobbyist can put 3-man years into programming, finding all bugs, documenting his product and distribute for free? The fact is, no one besides us has invested a lot of money in hobby software.
>
> (Gates 1976)

The letter writer was Bill Gates, who signed himself as 'General Partner, Micro-Soft' and would in later years become chief executive officer of Microsoft Corporation and, on the back of Microsoft's domination of operating systems and office software for personal computers, also the richest man in the world. While Gates' success at Microsoft might seem to confirm his view, he was quite wrong both in relation to his assertion that software must be treated as a particular kind of property and his claim that no-one would put years of work into writing and releasing professional quality software for free. The contradiction is the Free Software/Open Source movement.

Free Software/Open Source (FOSS) programming is based on an entirely different conception of the relationship between property and commerce to those the young Bill Gates argued were necessary. Later in this chapter, I will explore the complexities of this in detail, however at an introductory level we need to know that Free Software/Open Source[1] software is freely available; freedom here means that the programmes often need not be paid for but more importantly and fundamentally that the code that constitutes the software can be taken and adjusted for free as long as any changes made to the code are, in turn, made available to anyone else to use or adjust. It is important to note that as long as these latter conditions are met then FOSS code can be sold. Working year after working year has been poured into FOSS software producing operating systems like Linux, server software like Apache, fundamental Internet tools such as BIND, graphics programmes like GIMP or web browsers like Firefox. These software systems also play central roles, particularly in the backrooms that run the Internet. For example, Apache server software is used on around 60 per cent of all computers running web-servers, with its closest rival Microsoft claiming around 30 per cent (Netcraft 2007). The email systems Sendmail and Qmail subscribe, broadly, to Open Source and between them are likely to account for 80 per cent of email traffic (Bernstein 2003)[2]. The GNU Compiler has been for years the 'standard' compiler for many programmers. Elsewhere well-known programmes such as Linux or Firefox each have a much smaller market share but their complexity, stability and breadth demonstrate monumental programming efforts that are all debugged, documented and distributed for free, in utter and irrefutable contradiction of Bill Gates' 1976 expectation.

Not only was Gates wrong about people being willing to contribute their labour to freely distributed software programmes, he was also wrong about this free software preventing complex software being written for profit, as his personal fortune and the wealth of the company he co-founded attest. In some respects this argument may not be over, as so far FOSS software has not been able to compete as a desktop alternative, essentially due to difficulties over installation (now generally solved) and more latterly fears, now most likely unwarranted, over support for users of free software. A second, more fundamental, reason why FOSS programmes do not prevent programming for profit is that FOSS has itself produced profitable corporate models, as can be seen in companies such as Cygnus and Red Hat.

But we have moved into rather opaque waters; while nearly everyone is now familiar with software packages, computers and the Internet, we have moved to a point where simple, common-sense understandings will obscure rather than help introduce what is meant by hacking and the Free Software/Open Source movement. Before moving into the details of hacking and Open Source, we need to quickly establish something of what software means, particularly what software coding means and the difference between operating systems and other software.

Software consists of series of written instructions to the hardware components of a computer. These written instructions control everything the computer does, from drawing images on the screen to saving to files. Instructions which make up a programme that 'does' something, whether it be a word processor, spreadsheet, video game or any other, is called the 'source code' to that programme and is written in a particular language which defines what kinds of instructions exist and the syntax for those instructions (there are a number of these languages). These languages are themselves an abstraction laid over the top of the machinery of the computer and need to be translated into machine language to work. This translation is undertaken by programmes called compilers specifically designed for this task. Once compiled, a programme can run because the processor, that is the physical chip at the heart of the computer, can run sequences of two possible states – 0 or 1 – extremely fast. The compiler takes the source code written in a computer language and translates it into the machine language which is a massive series of '0s' and '1s' that a computer's hardware can understand.

There are, put very simply, two types of software programmes: operating systems and applications. Operating systems hum away constantly in the background, keeping all the different components of the computer, both hardware and software, running and in communication. Operating systems allocate memory, prioritise different tasks (such as printing while the music player, anti-virus and firewall continue to operate), managing files and generally keeping all components connected. Applications are programmes designed to perform particular functions such as a word processor, a spreadsheet or Internet browser. Applications themselves are usually bundles of different functions; a word processor includes a file saver, a print function, different fonts, and so on. Applications also depend on, or ride on top of, the operating system. One way of thinking of the difference is that applications directly perform actions the user of a computer wishes, such as writing these words, whereas an operating system integrates a computer's components to ensure uses of the computer are possible but does not itself perform such uses.

Though simple and somewhat short, these two descriptions of the nature of software and the two main types of software programmes are essential because the Free Software/Open Source movement is about writing software programmes. And writing such programmes is about a human being, somewhere, sitting down and typing instructions in a particular language to generate either an application or an operating system. The hackers we meet now hold conferences, argue in forums, create organisations, have meetings, write publicity and guides but above all, as the central defining feature of a FOSS hacker, they write software code. These hackers are deeply engaged in formulating network and computer technologies, they are focused on the creation of technical infrastructures that enable others to take certain actions – such as writing this chapter using a word processor. However, anything that creates opportunities also restrains and directs actions in certain ways. These hackers and their hacks both create technologies and grapple constantly with the constraints of technologies.

To understand the nature of Free Software/Open Source hacking we can break it down into three components: community, object and property.[3] Community refers to the way software is made. The FOSS community is a particular form of social organisation that creates the conditions for hackers to contradict Gates' assertions. The object refers to the moment when a particular technological determination made by FOSS hackers is temporarily closed. Objects refer to the social process of hacking a technological determination. Finally, property refers to the extension of technical hacking into social relations through novel definitions of property relations. This seeks to formalise the social relations of Open Source and, coincidentally, provide a vehicle for their extension outside technologies.

Community: many experts

The key to Free Software/Open Source is the commitment a hacker offers to software coding that is usually derived from some combination of three sources: intellectual challenge, fun and ideological commitment. A programmer can be challenged by the difficulty or complexity of a particular task. A programmer can see something as entertaining, taking up coding almost as a leisure activity (and often alongside a paid job). A programmer can believe in the necessity of free

software and the need to code a particular programme to support the movement. These three impulses to hack are sum-
marised by the Open Source mantra that good programming
comes from a programmer scratching an itch, that is, by a programmer working on a problem that is compelling to them. As
Weber puts it, 'The key element of the open source process, as
an ideal type, is voluntary participation and voluntary selection
of tasks' (Weber 2004: 62).

FOSS programmers choose what they work on, and usually
are volunteers. Even though as this type of software has grown
in importance, well-known programmers have increasingly
been employed by companies that are either themselves developing open source software or are willing to fund part of the
time of the employee for open source work. This is usually on
the premise that the open source programmer will continue
to choose their projects (often a programmer is employed
because of the work they have already done on a project that
they self-selected into). This is the first primary paradox, that
open source hackers freely choose their own tasks and from
this self-selection have come important and complex programmes. There are two models for how this development
proceeds, named by Open Source advocate Eric Raymond as
'the Cathedral and the Bazaar':

> I believed that the most important software (operating systems
> and really large tools like the Emacs programming editor)
> needed to be built like cathedrals, carefully crafted by individual
> wizards or small bands of mages working in splendid isolation,
> with no beta to be released before its time. . . . Linus Torvald's
> style of development – release early and often, delegate every-
> thing you can, be open to the point of promiscuity – came as a
> surprise. No quiet, reverent cathedral-building here – rather,
> the Linux community seemed to resemble a great babbling
> bazaar of differing agendas and approaches . . . out of which a
> coherent and stable system could seemingly emerge only by a
> succession of miracles. . . . The fact that this bazaar style
> seemed to work, and work well, came as a distinct shock.
>
> (Raymond 2001: 21–2)

Raymond is not here comparing open source with closed software development but two types of software development
within Free Software/Open Source. There are a number of leg-
endary hackers who are the model for Cathedral-type development; stereotypically, they are individuals who go on long
coding binges, or even a series of such binges, operating according to a plan hatched in their mind and spewed out through
typing fingers. Finally, they produce a programme others mar-
vel at both in terms of its capabilities and the elegance of its
design. Like a painter of genius, Cathedral developers appear to
miraculously produce, from private, almost secret, hours, complex and ingenious products which somehow fill a desire, sometimes even where no desire was previously perceived.

An example of such a developer is the founder of the Free
Software Foundation, Richard Stallman, who in Cathedral-like
fashion produced a number of fundamental software programmes, of which EMACS editing suite and the GNU C
Compiler (GCC) are the most frequently mentioned. As an
example of this kind of creativity, here is an account of part of
the production for EMACS of a better means of checking text
before printing (called 'pretty print') programmed by Stallman
with Guy Steele:

> 'We sat down one morning,' recalls Steele. 'I was at the key-
> board, and he was at my elbow,' says Steele. 'He was perfectly
> willing to let me type, but he was also telling me what to type.'
> The programming session lasted 10 hours. Throughout
> that entire time, Steele says, neither he nor Stallman took a
> break or made any small talk. By the end of the session, they
> had managed to hack the pretty print source code to just
> under 100 lines. 'My fingers were on the keyboard the whole
> time,' Steele recalls, 'but it felt like both our ideas were flow-
> ing onto the screen.'
>
> (Williams 2002: 87)

The only slightly unusual thing about this story is that it involves
two hackers rather than one and it continues in classic hacker
fashion with Steele only realising how much time has passed

when he goes outside to find it is dark. Such sudden leaps in programming can seem miraculous (indeed are sometimes as
close to miracles as any unbeliever is likely to find) because one
day something is unavailable and the next it is implemented.

Bazaar-style development is different, involving numbers of
programmers distributed across space, interacting through the
Internet to produce a complex piece of software. This model is
strongly dependent on the Internet to allow quick swapping of
feedback and files. The creation of Linux, the open source operating system kernel overseen by Linus Torvalds, is the best-
known example. One contributor, Rich Sladkey, remembered
the process this way:

> I discovered a bug. Since Linux came with source, my first
> inclination as a hacker was to take a look under the hood and
> see if I could fix the problem. I found that . . . I was able to
> navigate around the code pretty easily and provide a small
> patch to correct the problem.
>
> With my heart beating and my palms sweating, I com-
> posed the most professional message I could muster and sent
> it off to linus.torvalds@cs.helsinki.fi describing the bug and
> including my proposed fix. Minutes later he replied some-
> thing like, 'Yup, that's a bug. Nice investigation. Thanks.
> Fixed.' and I was hooked.
>
> (Moody 2001: 58)

Sladkey describes a process in which he can take the programme for Linux by downloading it over the Internet. He can
then inspect its inner workings because he has the source code
and is free to make changes. Once he spots a problem or bug,
he can change the programme, check that it works and then
send it back to Torvalds who can integrate it into a future
release of Linux. This latter point is the key one, for Sladkey
could have kept his modification to himself or could have
posted up an alternative version of Linux including his change
and making himself the controller. As will be discussed later in
this chapter, the process of ensuring any changes are released
to one and all is controlled through the licence under which

Linux is provided but there is nothing to stop Sladkey keeping the change secret or producing Sladkey-Linux. The fact that Sladkey improved the code and returned the gift allowed Torvalds to produce a better version of Linux that then bene-fited many people while also ensuring developers kept produc-ing a common product. Torvalds described his decision to become the co-ordinator of this process as almost accidental:

> Linus explains his viewpoint on these early bug fixes. 'They started out so small, that I never got the feeling that, hey, how dare they impose on my system. Instead, I just said, OK, that's right, obviously correct, and so in it went [to the kernel]. The next time it was much easier, because at that time there weren't many people who did this, so I got to know the people who sent in changes. And again they grew gradually, and so at no point I felt, hey, I'm losing control.'
>
> (Moody 2001: 58)

With these simplified versions of the two programming processes of the Cathedral and the Bazaar now before us, we can see already the centrality of community and the way the constitution of the community supporting each programme also constitutes the process by which a programme is produced and developed. For example, Apache is one of the great FOSS success stories, being the software used to define how over 60 per cent of computers serving web pages can do so. Apache emerged when eight developers, all already employed to create and maintain worldwide web services, came together to try and develop better software. Quickly Apache developed into a struc-ture with hundreds of developers. Beginning with an informal process of generating consensus on developments using email, this system soon began to buckle under the pressure of increas-ing numbers of developers, none of whom could be sure exactly when they would be available for their Apache work, only that they would at some point be available. The result was a system of email voting based on voting rights for any participating developer but with only decisions voted on by the Apache Group members being binding. Becoming an Apache Group member is by nomination from an existing member and then ratified only by a unanimous vote (Weber 2004: 186–8).

Apache represents a different model of decision making to Linux but it is also built on the large-scale involvement of developers. The key difference is that there is a formal decision-making structure which makes the community visible in institutional terms. In contrast, Linux continued to develop in informal ways, with the most obvious and important development being the emergence of 'lieutenants' who took control of particular parts of Linux, feeding changes in their area up to Torvalds who maintains overall co-ordination.

Whether through the productions of individuals contributing major sections of code or through widely dispersed networks of developers, whether formally or informally organised, FOSS programmes produce and rely upon communities because the software is open to collaborative, dispersed development. The edges of such communities begin to include non-programmers in activities such as reporting failures or bugs in programmes or helping to write 'how-to' guides or documentation. However, such communities only exist because of the participation of programmers, and this fundamentally marks out the hacker nature of Free Software/Open Source through programmers' constant struggle to determine and redetermine software technologies.

This also allows a further delimitation of this hacking community and an important limitation of Raymond's metaphor to be identified. As Weber argues, Raymond suggests the bazaar works because he assumes all the resources needed to make it work are plentiful, but this is incorrect. In a situation where data can be constantly and instantly transferred there is no end of changes to source code that can be created and passed to others who, in turn, will make improvements and share them, leading to an exponential increase in the quality of programmes. But this assumes a plentiful supply of what is actually a scarcity in good programming expertise. Weber argues Free Software/Open Source are communities built on expertise, they include cultures of what is the good and bad exercise of expertise and they exclude the vast majority of people on the basis of their inability to programme (Weber 2004: 54–93). This is no bad thing; the idea is that someone who is good at programming should be able to find a place within collaborative efforts to programme, with the products of this effort openly available to users and other programmers alike. But this introduces a general scarcity that looks like the opposite from within the community; not many people can programme well enough to make a difference to FOSS programmes but nearly all FOSS community members are programmers.

The assumption that the bazaar can flourish only works from within the hacking community because it is only within that community that it makes any sense to assume that programming expertise is plentiful. This opens up a further objection as bazaars do not produce a single object, they produce a process of market interaction, but at any point in the FOSS community what is produced is an object that is susceptible to a reasonably crude measure of success: does it run?

Does it run? Objects and the importance of methods of closure

While we can see communities of programmers organised in different ways and both promoting and being subjected to different methods of decision making, we should not lose sight of the object. Each Free Software/Open Source project is based on a product, a software programme or a part of a software programme. This programme also forms the means of measuring that project or, put another way, the success of that community. And each such product is subject to a remarkably simple test: does the software run? Does the software do what it says it will? We can see this when considering the conditions under which Linux began to make its way in the world, which requires a brief detour into computer history.

Way back in the dark ages of computers there was an operating system called Unix, which was made freely available by the telephone company that owned it, AT&T, because that company had been accused of monopolistic practices by the US government (under Eisenhower in the 1950s), and had settled the action through a legally binding declaration that it would not participate in commercial activities outside its telephony business. Software, being outside of telephony could not be a commercial activity for AT&T, despite Unix being developed at its Bell Laboratories (Weber 2004: 22, 28–9). Unix was therefore distributed free, with a licence but also with its source code, encouraging programmers to tinker with it and develop alternatives. Variants of Unix developed, proliferating from the late 1970s. AT&T's legally binding declaration was altered significantly due to a second anti-monopoly action in the early 1980s, which had wide-ranging effects by breaking up telephone monopolies but which also freed AT&T to charge for non telephony-based business activities, meaning it could charge for Unix. AT&T had always distributed a licence claiming ownership of the software but it had also always distributed it for free (because it had to) and with the source code. In the early 1980s, it began to charge and to withhold the source code. At the same time, variants of Unix, written and re-written by various people, continued to proliferate breaking Unix up into a wide range of programmes that spread programmer efforts thinly. Not only was there significant confusion between such versions but Unix's legal owners began to sue those it felt were stealing its software and reusing it. The availability of a free operating system complete with source code appeared to be disappearing.

Into this increasingly complicated quagmire of legal and coding issues, came the announcement that the Free Software Foundation, the organisation Richard Stallman co-founded to fight for free access to programmes and their source code, would develop from scratch a free operating system; free as in free culture, complete with source code. A great many tools relevant to any operating system already existed as part of the FSF or GNU software suite; including the much loved and admired text editor EMACS, a powerful compiler in GCC and other key building blocks. But a central component was missing, the butler in the middle who organised all the different software components and kept the whole software system coordinated and speaking coherently to the hardware; what is called the kernel. FSF announced a project to write a freely available kernel called Hurd and proceeded to try and do so in the early 1990s. However, Hurd did not appear for years and years despite significant effort by programmers at the Free Software Foundation (Williams 2002: 142–3).

The scene is set, Act 1 concludes with the venerable Unix beloved of programmers struck down by, on the one hand, the demands of private property and profit who wielded the twin daggers of licences and lawyers and, on the other hand, the querulousness of its own lovers who argued among themselves producing ever more and ever more confusing distinctions between versions of Unix. The FSF hero who would rescue a free operating system announced itself in the determination to add a kernel to the GNU software suite, but this hero then proceeded to ride in circles rather than to the rescue. Act 1 has the damsel in distress, a cast of evil attackers, confused lovers and an ineffective hero. Act 2 shifts scene entirely as an unexpected and seemingly insignificant move is made by a young gentleman whose name is Linus Torvalds and whose kernel is called Linux. The weakling that Torvalds produced was first neglected by the expected hero Hurd, with Stallman hearing about Torvalds' fledgling programme and, understandably, delegating to someone else the responsibility of assessing it. When the report came back detailing some technical difficulties, the Hurd team missed the wood for the trees by not taking into account that despite the difficulties Torvalds' project actually ran – it worked (Williams 2002: 145).

We do not need to follow the ins and outs of a play that continues to be written to this day, but we can see the unexpected opportunity and in Torvalds' case an opportunity he did not know about and had not in any clear way identified. What many programmers needed was a kernel that ran, that was stable even if primitive. Torvalds provided this as the result almost of an accidental, and he thought, possibly passing obsession with programming. Torvalds had been using and exploring computers in detail from early on in life. By 1991 (exactly at the point when Hurd had been announced for a while but was running into programming sands) he acquired a new computer and used it to run a version of Unix called Minix. This was a Unix-like operating system created for teaching purposes. One thing Minix did not do well, at least in Torvalds' view, was terminal emulation – which is a way of providing a window on the screen which allows commands to be executed on a different computer. Torvalds wanted to connect to his university's computer from home for various reasons and Minix did not do that well. He says:

> So I began a project to create my own terminal emulation program. I didn't want to do the project under Minix, but instead to do it at the bare hardware level. This terminal emulation project would also be a great opportunity to learn how the 386 hardware worked. As I mentioned, it was winter in Finland.
> (Torvalds with Diamond 2001: 62)

Torvalds used his existing expertise to explore his new computer, in pursuit of a programme he needed. He added more and more features as it began to work for him, and it began to do things that made it seem a bit more than just a terminal emulator. For example, he wished to upload and download files between the university and home computers but for that he needed to be able to save to disk. This in turn meant writing a range of fundamental computer operations concerning file systems and organisation, such as making the files he saved from his terminal compatible with the Minix operating system so that he could look at those files when not using his custom terminal.

By the time I did this it was clear the project was on its way to becoming an operating system. So I shifted my thinking of it as a terminal emulator to thinking of it as an operating system. I think the transition occurred in the hypnosis of one of those marathon programming sessions. Day or night? I can't recall. One moment I'm in my threadbare robe hacking away on a terminal emulator with extra functions. The next moment I realize it's accumulating so many functions that it has metamorphosed into a new operating system in the works.

(Cited in Torvalds with Diamond 2001: 78)

At this stage, Torvalds asked in a online forum about some standards he needed to implement as part of his kernel and not long after began posting versions of his programe into a space that anyone could take a copy from over the Internet. Torvalds' obsessive programming led him to constantly integrate changes but what captured interest immediately, and led to a quick increase in programmers' contributions, was that Torvalds' programme worked; from the start, Linux ran. A systems programmer and Minix-user Derek Leiber said:

'As for the code quality [of early Linux], I guess I thought it was mediocre.' But mediocre or not, he adds, 'I was amazed that it worked. I'd expected that I'd get it installed, watch it crash, and move on. But the damned thing actually ran. I don't think I pushed it too hard, but I don't remember ever crashing it. Even in the early days.'

(Moody 2001: 55–6)

Torvalds had written Linux so that it could co-exist, in different areas, on the same hard drive as Microsoft's DOS-Windows operating system (legend has it he did so in order to ensure he could continue playing the computer game Prince of Persia) allowing people to try Linux without having to lose their current system. I have already quoted Rich Sladkey as a developer of Linux, here is his description of his first involvement:

The idea of a free compiler with the quality of GCC, already well established at the time, and a free hosting OS [operating system] supporting a full multi-tasking Unix environment was attractive. So attractive it had to be tried to see if it could be real. . . . from my very first installation, Linux was dramatically more stable than my co-resident installation of Windows 3.1 on top of MS-DOS 5.

(Cited in Moody 2001: 57)

Many report their interest in Linux and other Free Software/ Open Source projects as being about the utility of the programme: I needed to do such a thing and this programme almost did it so I became enamoured and contributed. What is sometimes forgotten is that the programme has to run in some way for contributions to be solicited. According to Raymond, you cannot start a bazaar-like project in the bazaar, you have to have something to begin with:

> When you start community-building, what you need to be able to present is a plausible promise. Your programme doesn't have to work particularly well. It can be crude, buggy, incomplete, and poorly documented. What it must not fail to do is (a) run, and (b) convince potential co-developers that it can be evolved into something really neat in the foreseeable future.
>
> (Raymond 2001: 47)

The key to the issue of 'does it run' is that a test is available by which development can be guided. Consider some people collaboratively writing a poem or painting a painting and how they will be able to work on its development. Of course, people sometimes manage to do this, but rarely and only in very small numbers. This is perhaps mainly because there are no clear criteria for what is successful or good. Software programmes collaboratively developed, dependent on communities of contributors, can be organised in a number of ways, some administratively tight and some loose, but they have the advantage of an object whose success or failure can, at any one moment, be put to the test.

What constitutes success may be fiercely contested; someone may argue that a programme does not 'run' if it does not have certain features or if it does not run on certain hardware or if it is not elegant, or some other criteria. This continues to point us in the direction of the collaborative nature of Free Software/Open Source communities. Within them, certain standards will be used to judge programmes. What are thought to be the 'principles' of Unix culture are often behind such judgements. These principles tend towards a philosophy of building in small, simple, modular programmes that do one thing well and which are able to be connected to other similar programmes each also doing one thing well (Weber 2004: 25–7). Here is the often quoted codification of Unix culture enunciated by one of the early Unix programmers Doug McIlroy:

> This is the Unix philosophy:
> Write programmes that do one thing and do it well.
> Write programmes to work together.
> Write programmes to handle text streams because that is a universal interface.
>
> (Cited in Wikipedia 2007)

Yet even within shared norms and cultures which allow the judging of software and within collaborative communities built on easy and ubiquitous communication between members, FOSS has a way of focusing judgements by defining a fragile moment in which a programme will 'run' or not. As we saw with Linux, it succeeded because it emerged into a particular moment which allowed its worth to be seen and it had no clear competitor but it also succeeded through the crucial step of running and continuing to run.

It is not so much that the 'running' of a programme by itself solves debates but that it provides a framework within which hackers can argue about how to close a debate. There are arguments of the type 'it runs but it's ugly', destabilising the notion of a successful programme, or there are programmes that can be supported even though they do not run because they show great promise or fit an important niche. Hurd provides an example of a programme that did not run but which received serious programming attention because it was expected to fill an important role. Rather, the success of the object is a way in which a community can define a test. The nature of what it means to 'run' may be negotiated but at some point different people will take that object, the programme, and use it. Again, Hurd is an important example because though it did not run and it did receive support, the 'does it run?' question finally came to haunt it. Even with basic functionality early Linux progressed because it ran, showing that 'running' can trump grand designs or impressive institutional backing. This is not because such things as designs and institutions are not attractive to hackers but because they will move to whatever seems most promising to hack on. And once a programme begins to attract serious hacking attention, in part because it runs, then it will begin to move ahead, gradually becoming the programme that everyone wanted in the first place.

We have seen how a community builds technological objects, keeping them simultaneously always open and always closed. We have seen how the object that is the programme that can run, allows opportunities to be defined around which communities revolve. We now need to consider more closely what holds these processes together, and what keeps them fluid. We have seen that a problem for Unix was that when ownership was asserted the object was no longer clearly, freely available. So far I have not pointed out that Minix was under the same constraint and so Torvalds could not simply hack on it. Minix was licensed by its owner, who wished to keep control so that Minix would retain its character as a teaching tool. Notions of property are involved in the collaborations of Free Software/Open Source projects and we need to add to community and the object, the nature of property, to finish an overview of FOSS hackers.

Property: exclusion versus distribution

It might seem strange to turn to property after community and object, because we might expect the nature of property to be

defined by these things and so to be a rather trivial consequence instead of an independent component. Such a thought
really refers us not to the primary causality of any one of the
three elements of Free Software/Open Source but to a realisa-
tion that whatever is discussed last of the three will appear to
be a consequence of the other two and that any of the three
might have been discussed last. In my account, property is an
appropriate third because, in many ways, it summarises and
encompasses the movement; so much so that acute observers
have been led to define the Free Software/Open Source movement on the basis of a particular form of property rights.
'Open source is an experiment in social organization for production around a distinctive notion of property. . . . Property in
open source is configured fundamentally around the right to
distribute, not the right to exclude' (Weber 2004: 16). Property
relations are structured by communities that then rely on
those notions of property, usually supported by extensive puni-
tive mechanisms for not conforming to predefined property
forms. Free Software/Open Source develops a novel form of
property but, as Weber implies, the normal concept of property
in late twentieth-century over-developed nations needs to be
kept in mind.

The type of property assumed by Free Software/Open
Source defines an object and then confers exclusive rights to
that object onto some entity, usually a person, group or organisation. We are familiar with this; consider buying a newspaper. I walk into a shop and there is a pile of newspapers, one of
which I want. The shop seems to have an abundance of these
things so perhaps I should just consider it my right to take one.
However, being aware of the customs and laws of the nation I
live in, I take a newspaper and then offer money to the shop-
keeper, who takes the money and waves me on my way. Now I
have a pile of newsprint that is mine and which I would be very
unhappy to have taken away from me: though, because it is
mine, I might offer to share it or give it to someone. The property is exclusive to the owner. This kind of property is enforced

by a wide range of institutions, including law courts and the police who will, when properly provoked, ensure that I be put in jail or fined if I do not conform to the rights of exclusive property.

Free Software, and then Open Source, do not deny the essentials of the concept of property just outlined. This is key, as both movements are sometimes mistakenly believed to have overturned the notion of property. Instead, the well-known and legally enforceable notion of property as exclusive rights is simultaneously reinforced and inverted. The fundamental idea is that, if it is my right to control my property then I can define under what conditions others can use my property, and if I define those conditions specifically enough then my property should remain the property of all who wish to use it. Moreover, I can define my property in such a way that others are legally bound to make any alterations they make to my property freely available to others. Instead of controlling my property by focusing on my exclusive rights to it, I can instead enforce this right and make my property a freely available entity, making sure that no-one else has a right to exclude others from my property.

The inversion came about in this way. It may be hard to remember in our software-dominated societies but there was a time when there seemed few commercial applications for software. Even if people could see, in theory, that software was something that could be bought and sold, there were so few computers and these were generally in the hands of programmers themselves, that software tended to be freely exchanged. This history, or rather this arcadian memory of the programmer's paradise lost, fuels the belief that there was once an accidental programming community that swapped and shared software with a view to producing the best software. But as computers grew in importance, commercial opportunities blossomed and the free distribution of software was questioned. Many programmers moved from universities to companies and often also signed non-disclosure agreements

ensuring they could no longer even talk about their programming to anyone outside their corporation.

Richard Stallman noted not the financial opportunities software commercialisation offered but the community destruction it caused. Stallman's community of programmers had
been based on software exchange and was broken as individuals moved on to corporate jobs and software became closed. He
explored writing and giving back software to keep the computers he was working with open, but issues began to arise over
what might happen to his software. Stallman's strategy was to
distribute software he had written, and so initially owned, with
a licence that not only allowed others to use and modify his
programme but that also ensured they acted the same way in
turn. To do this he realised he had to close off the escape hatch
by which someone could take his programme, modify it and
then issue it with a restrictive licence. Stallman and colleagues
came up with a solution they called copyleft, which Stallman
explained in this way:

> The goal of GNU was to give users freedom, not just to be
> popular. So we needed distribution terms that would prevent
> GNU software from being turned into proprietary software.
> The method we use is called 'copyleft'. . . . The central idea of
> copyleft is that we give everyone permission to run the pro-
> gram, copy the program, modify the program, and distribute
> modified versions – but not permission to add restrictions of
> their own. Thus, the crucial freedoms that define 'free soft-
> ware' are guaranteed to everyone who has a copy; they
> become inalienable rights.
>
> (Stallman 1999: 59)

This goal needed to be carefully codified. For example, see this
similarly spirited licence written for a programme called trn in
1985 by programmer Larry Wall.

> Copyright © 1985, Larry Wall
> You may copy the trn kit in whole or in part as long as you
> don't try to make money off it, or pretend that you wrote it.
> (Cited in Williams 2002: 125)

The Free Software Foundation developed a less informal and legally binding version of copyleft so that, as Weber argues, the normal sense of property is inverted from 'the right to exclude you from using something that belongs to me. Property in open source is configured fundamentally around the right to distribute, not the right to exclude' (Weber 2004: 1). This desire was codified into the GNU Public License (GPL), which has been through three versions. We need not go into the legal specificities of the GPL, rather it is important to see the work that the GPL does and to know that it has been progressively developed to make it as binding as seems possible in legal contexts (see chapter 5 for further discussion).

The desire to reconfigure property as distribution rather than exclusion is built from a community impulse – from the desire to embody a programming community in legal language to ensure the property relations of exclusion do not undermine the existence of free exchange necessary for that community. In this context we can make the property relations at work clearer by noting that selling an open source programme is entirely permitted. The problem is not in selling property but in selling property which includes changes that are not freely shared back to the programming community. Stallman partly funded his early period of free software work by selling tapes of his EMAC and GCC programmes. Billion-dollar companies such as Red Hat or Suse have grown through selling versions of Linux, and have funded programmers who have contributed back to free software. Some projects are also run from within companies, who act as their co-ordinator. As the slogan goes: free as in free culture, not as in free beer. There is no contradiction in free software being sold, in fact the licences were designed to ensure this was possible.

The complexity of this type of licence is that it retains the notion of exclusion, it remains a definition within traditional notions of private property, but it uses exclusion to promote distribution. The GPL, and other similar licences, exclude anyone who uses copylefted software from using exclusion instead of distribution as their principle of property rights. Distribution becomes the primary property right, but distribution is only secured by relying on the longstanding legal right to exclude users from property someone owns. The Free Software/Open Source community, or at least those within that community who apply GPL-like licences to their software, relies on exclusion to establish distribution. Free Software/Open Source is not about finance, it is about the right to access and change software combined with the responsibility to give back any changes.

Free Software/Open Source movement

This is a movement of experts. It is a movement of (mainly) professional programmers and documentation writers, of website operators and weekend coders, of publicists and innovative lawyers, of ideologues and pragmatists; above all, it is a movement that uses collective action to grapple constantly and directly with the nature of software and the technological determinations that exist, might exist and have been overcome in software.

We can see how this movement explodes the notion of technological determinism that has for so long been threaded through social sciences and most popular discussions of society and technology. The fact that at any specific point in time everyone will be, in some way or other, technologically determined is taken for granted. Further, the fact that all technologies are malleable and open to social and cultural determinations is also taken for granted. These two positions are usually taken as mutually exclusive, as opponents in a battle for a true understanding of the nature of relations between technology and society, but they are not so in hacking. Instead, hacking reveals them as complementary sides of the constant process of determinations that characterise technologies that are always already present in societies.

Free Software/Open Source is characterised by a creative

engagement with software that flows through the nature of its community, its ability to socially mediate conclusions through the nature of the software object and by its inversion of property relations to ensure distribution is primary. Hacking reaches some of its clearest and most idealistic moments in this movement. The figure of Richard M. Stallman embodies this idealism and the conflicts it may produce. The figure of Linus Torvalds shows where such idealism may produce a framework within which pragmatists can create the most remarkable feats of software production, by drawing not on individual genius but the collective action of individual sourcerers, geniuses, malcontents and even some mediocrities. All of these people write code for freedom.

Notes

1 Free Software and Open Source are different things, as will be discussed in Chapter 5. However, for the purposes of this overview they are similar enough to be presented together. I will use FOSS to represent Free Software and Open Source Software.
2 Figures for Sendmail and Qmail are drawn into the controversy over the security of Sendmail. However, from figures available, 80 per cent is their approximate market share.
3 This division is derived from Weber (2004) who suggests property, community and politics. My change is based on the contention that politics permeates property and community to such an extent it cannot be separated and that the role of the object is underestimated by Weber. But, at the same time, my account is deeply indebted to Weber's pioneering work.

CHAPTER FOUR

Hacking the Social: Hacktivism, Cyberwar, Cyberterror, Cybercrime

The community of hacking

Community is a much used word these days in popular politics, with references to 'the community' dropping from the lips of almost anyone concerned with social and cultural issues. There is also a theoretical tradition in the social sciences examining community, which is almost entirely ignored by the popular usage of 'community'. This social science tradition has in recent years been absorbed into theories taking up the nature of community: from Anderson's (1983) exploration of 'collective imaginations', through social movement analyses of collective actions to Bourdieu's notion of the habitus or Barnes' work on agency. So far, it has not been necessary to ask what is meant by 'community' when referring to the hacking community, rather it has been important to show what hackers do.

This has led us to see two major components of hacking in crackers and Free Software/Open Source who both engage with software technologies in ways that establish and contest determination of actions by computer and network technologies. Moreover, both contest these determinations in ways that explode existing understandings of technological determination. Rather than taking part in a contest between technological determinations of society or social determinations of technology they enter into both as two sides of the one nature of social technologies. We have before us a technologically mediated community, if ever there was one and, unsurprisingly, it teaches us something about the nature of technology and society. Technology is never asocial and society is never atechnological, and at any moment each is able to be both determined by and be determining, the other.

For hackers, software technologies are important conditions for taking social and cultural action. What action any person may take is conditioned by the technologies surrounding the desired action, both in terms of the range of actions that are possible and the nature of each possible action. And these social and cultural actions can just as often be the redetermination of a technology as they may be something directed away from technology. This explosion of technological determinism from a contest between society and technology into the melding of the two without losing the fact of determination, is the hallmark of hacking as a community.

Having established this view of hacking, it is no longer possible to avoid the question: what is meant by community? For many, communities are based on a notion of collective identity; that is, a sense of a 'we' or an identity that is informally negotiated between community members. Similarly, I might invoke, as Taylor and I have done previously, the concept of the imagined community, which is imagined because not all members of the community can meet and so they must imagine their relationship with each other, but yet can create a community because of a deep sense of non-hierarchical comradeship between members (Melucci 1996; Anderson 1983; Jordan and Taylor 1998). The definition of community is a complex area of debate, however the definitions I have just given are in their own way well established and provide the basis for a brief discussion of what community might mean in relation to hacking (Studdert 2005).

Definitions based on the concepts of collective identity and imagined communities focus on the dynamic processes by which communities are created and maintained, both requiring constant work and change but at the same time yielding up particular practices by which a constantly changing community can be defined. Barry Barnes captures this sense of how different actions produce something that might be called sameness, or a communal norm:

> The successful execution of routine social practices always involves the continual overriding of routine practices (habits, skills) at the individual level. Think of an orchestra playing a familiar work or a military unit engaged in a march-past. Any description of these activities as so many agents each following the internal guidance of habit or rule would merely describe a fiasco. Individual habituated competence is of course necessary in these contexts, but so too is a constant active intervention to tailor individual performances to what other participants are doing, always bearing in mind the goal of the overall collective performance. . . . It is the product of the interaction of social agents constantly adjusting and aligning what otherwise would be non-identical and incongruous individual performances. It is the continuing consequence not of sameness and aggregations, but of difference and sociability.
>
> (Barnes 2000: 55–6)

Hacking needs to be defined by a series of commonly enacted interactions or material practices which both create and wrap around hacking techniques. These practices can be described as routine but only in Barnes' sense of routine which understands how different individual practices constantly adjust against each other to construct a routine or, in this case, a norm which in turn constitutes a community. The hack (and crack) remain the central material practices but a range of other factors need to be recognised as a basis for a community, without which individual hacks would remain just that – odd and isolated moments rather than instances of widely significant social and cultural trends.

Dispersed individuals, many of whom may never meet, construct and give allegiance to a community by taking actions through which they recognise some as part of their community and others as outside that community. This is a dispersed notion of community, not relying on physical co-location, but instead emphasising the fluidity of people's ongoing construction of their social and cultural norms, and all this in contexts where people can be expected to be part of several communities at any one time. One expression of this dispersed and malleable community constructed not so much by structures as by social practices was given by the hacker Marotta in an interview. He claimed: 'To find "hacker culture" you have to take a very wide view of the cyberspace terrain and watch the interactions among physically diversified people who have in common a mania for machines and software. What you will find will be a gossamer framework of culture' (Marotta cited in Jordan and Taylor 1998: 762).

This gossamer framework includes more than just the crackers and open sourcerors that we have already identified. We can give some structure to an emerging sense of a networked and dispersed community by noting that though these two groups provide the core of hacking, a wide range of closely related groups, each with their own sense of identity, flow around and through them. The full richness of hacking can now emerge because we have followed through the nature of its most important exponents allowing us now to pay attention to related actions and groups. And there are many hackers other than crackers and open sourcerors, who we can now identify. I will fill these in, though of necessity more briefly than I have cracking and Free Software/Open Source.

These floating identities can be grouped into two themes: hacking the social; and programming, non-hacking and cultures of hacking. These are called themes because they are not constituted by material proximities or connections – the same people actually talking to the same people – but are grouped around a common use of hacking, producing a particular form of identity. Within each of these themes we will find several groups, some of which relate closely to each other and others of which do not. The groups I outline are neither entirely stable nor entirely institutionalised, but reflect long-standing identities that have multiple connections.

The idea of identities is appropriate here both for the ability of identities to change and the ability of individuals to take on more than one identity at a time. The hackers about to be identified should not be thought of as individuals who are mutually exclusive and can participate only in one of these identities. Rather, just as a cracker can be an open sourceror and vice versa, so many of the identities I am about to outline can be taken up by the same person at the same time, or be passed through over different times. These are 'subject-positions' not lifelong, fixed identities.

Hackers and their characteristic techniques and ethos have been taken outside of the software-fuelled virtual world. This is not the same as the fact that hacking directly creates aspects of our world, the need for computer security or the speed of Internet communication, for example. Rather I am referring to people who take hacking's particular approach to both collapsing and recreating a social/technology distinction outside the production of software or the manipulation of computers and networks.

Here we find a range of attempts to apply hacking to particular aspects of 'the social'. The latter term, the 'social', is appropriate here as I am not dealing with 'society' but with various aspects of the way we live in twenty-first-century societies. These forms of hacking do not address either the whole of something called society nor do they deal with just society – addressing as they do politics and economics among other things – thus they address aspects of 'the social' in the following areas: grassroots or popular political activism, conflict between nation-states, the nature of security and terror and shifting forms of crime.

Hacktivism: activists in the virtual

The politics of hacking has so far been about technological determinism. Cracking and Free Software/Open Source politics share a concern to engage closely with the nature of computers and networks, breaking them open for manipulation while creating further objects which can at any particular moment be closed to social intervention. This is a politics that assumes no fundamental distinction between social and technological yet also assumes determinisms between them and which applies these assumptions to the production, manipulation and transfer of information.

Hacktivism is produced by taking forward the collapse of a technological-social distinction in computer and network technologies and applying it to politics outside of the information-soaked spaces created by computers and networks. Hacktivism takes cracking and open source techniques and cultures and applies them to the politics that dominate the front pages of our newspapers – globalisation, human rights, ecology – rather than the politics that dominate discussion in the backrooms of IT support.

Hacktivism emerged in the mid 1990s in a combination of theoretical and practical initiatives in the context of the emerging anti or alter-globalisation movement. Groups such as the Critical Arts Ensemble called for electronic civil disobedience to confront the powers-that-be in the emerging networked world. 'At one time the control of the streets *was* a valued item. . . . capital has become increasingly decentralized, breaking through national boundaries and abandoning cities, street action has become increasingly useless' (CAE 1996: 11). And if the streets are now useless for protesting against power because power resides in the global information network then protest needs to adjust:

> As in CD [civil disobedience], the primary tactics in ECD [electronic civil disobedience] are trespass and blockage. Exits, entrances, conduits and other key spaces must be occupied by the contestational force in order to bring pressure on legitimized institutions engaged in unethical or criminal actions. Blocking information conduits is analogous to blocking physical locations.
>
> (CAE 1996: 18)

Such theories were beginning to be matched by practice as groups such as Netstrike, Electronic Disturbance Theater

(EDT) and the Electrohippies began to explore ways of blocking electronic streets. A key tactic was the insight that by bombarding a target on the Internet with enough information the target becomes overloaded and either crashes, disappearing from cyberspace, or is at least badly slowed down (Jordan and Taylor 2004: 69–74). Netstrike put this into practice in the simplest possible way, requesting that at a certain time all protesters put the target url into their browser and press the reload button repeatedly. Both EDT and the Electrohippies developed automated tools for creating such demonstrations, with EDT releasing their tool and making it widely available. The Electrohippies ran perhaps the most emblematic such protest by creating an online attack on the computer networks serving the World Trade Organisation conference in Seattle in 1999. This was the moment when the alter-globalisation movement burst into public view, and during classic civil disobedience tactics involving struggle in the streets to prevent delegates attending the conference, there were attempts to clog up the Internet connections to the conference, slowing down and halting the conference network (Jordan and Taylor 2004: 74–9). CD and ECD joined in the one action protesting against an organisation accused of fomenting exploitation through its programme of 'neo-liberal globalisation'.

Such actions pose a problem however because the multiplication of information on the Internet is far easier than the multiplication of bodies on a street. One person can sit at a computer connection and through the magic of software produce a flood of information. In this way, such premier sites as Ebay and Amazon have been summarily removed from the Internet. Hacktivism that takes mass action must distinguish itself in some way from denial of service attacks because such attacks can be launched by one or a few people. This is a problem for hacktivism because it is recreating civil disobedience and takes over the underlying sense of legitimacy civil disobedience gains from numbers of bodies. A blockage on the streets, a boycott or a street protest, all rely for their legitimacy on the numbers of bodies that support the action (Jordan 2002: 53–69). This form of political legitimacy is taken over by electronic civil disobedience (ECD) but creates a very different political problem when applied to the Internet.

Whereas the problem for civil disobedience is attracting bodies, leading to logistical issues, the problem for electronic civil disobedience is what counts as a legitimate political body. In a realm where streams of information can be produced at the touch of a button, how can electronic civil disobedience ensure that the information targeted at a site is generated by many people and not by software? Electronic civil disobedience begins to work against the technological capabilities of the Internet in order to ensure its protests are seen as politically legitimate; in the process ECD produces a form of hacking which seeks less than optimal technological performance (Jordan and Taylor 2004: 79–82). ECD actions have done this by implementing technologies which utilise only a little multiplication. Netstrike's instruction to repeatedly click on the reload button is the most extreme example of this, with each request to the target meant to represent one protester's click on a button. Both Electronic Disturbance Theater and the Electrohippies developed technologies which automatically reload their target over and over again, allowing the protester to start the action but then to leave it; both also allowed the one protester to initiate several connections, though not so many as to undermine the legitimacy of the protest. However it is done, the technologies of electronic civil disobedience must establish the political legitimacy of the bodies that are protesting, or be accused of being the actions of isolated individuals using software multiplication.

A second type of hacktivism emerged simultaneously with electronic civil disobedience and focused hacking onto protecting and extending the availability of information on the Internet. These hacktivists valued the Internet's ability to distribute information freely to a wide range of people and became concerned at attempts to control or limit such distribution.

Such controls could target either the availability of information, for example in such things as national firewalls that monitor Internet traffic into and out of a particular nation-state and are capable of blocking particular sites, or through tracking individuals who access particular bits of information and then arresting or disciplining them. These informational hacktivists are concerned to ensure free secure access to information.

These hacktivists tend toward the production of software which, when embedded in the Internet, will defeat attempts to limit access to information or to identify whoever is attempting to access information. For example, Hacktivismo (self-described as 'a group of international hackers, human rights workers, artists and others who seek to further the goals of human rights through technology' (Hacktivismo 2006)), released in September 2006 a portable, anonymous web browser. This browser can be used from a memory stick and employs various technical means, such as changing Internet protocol (ip) address frequently, to ensure that the user's identity cannot be traced on the Internet or on the specific computer being used. The press release went on to quote one of Hacktivismo's founders, Oxblood Ruffin, on the reasons for releasing Torpark. 'We live in a time where acquisition technologies are cherry picking and collating every aspect of our online lives. Torpark continues Hacktivismo's commitment to expanding privacy rights on the Internet. And the best thing is, it's free. No one should have to pay for basic human rights, especially the right of privacy' (Hacktivismo 2006).

Torpark relies on a further innovation of informational hacktivists: the Tor network. Tor is a distributed computer network aiming to provide protection against various means of tracking people's online habits. It consists of clouds of interconnected computers, each running Tor's own server software. When someone makes a request to a Tor server that request provokes the creation of a 'virtual circuit', which is a series of Tor servers randomly joined to each other through encrypted connections for a short time. The requests then travel through this circuit, which is broken down and remade at frequent intervals. In this way various means of tracking identity through the Internet can be at least severely obstructed, if not prevented.

The politics here relies particularly on Free Software/Open Source methods. This is in two ways, one technical and one political. Technically the development of such software is done in similar fashion to the development of any FOSS package, employing all the facets of Free Software/Open Source explored already in chapter 3. The political factor is that access to the source code means that many eyes can check software for any hidden or unwanted political determinations. For example, in early 2007 some security analysts released a paper suggesting ways of breaking the Tor network and of tracking people and their online histories even when using Tor. A series of online discussions followed, one of which included the following response to a blog arguing that Tor is still safe. The poster claimed, 'Did you know Tor was openly created by the NSA (and promoted by the EFF)? Did you know Tor is NSA spyware, created by spooks, just like Freenet?' (Anon 2007).[1] The sting in this is that while Tor was not initially developed by the US government's National Security Agency, it had been developed by the US Navy's Naval Research Lab. An immediate response by the executive director of the Tor Project, Shava Nerad, pointed out that:

> Um. Do you know that Tor was openly designed by the Naval Research Lab, who sent it out into the world as open source?
>
> Do you know that, as open source, Tor can't have any backdoors, because there are thousands of programmers all over the world who look at the code and understand it?
>
> (Anon 2007)

The defence against accusations that Tor had been infiltrated, if not initiated in the manner of a virtual agent provocateur, by US security agencies is that it does not matter where the software comes from because it is open source and so has been and can be at any time inspected by vigilant programmers. The politics of hacktivists for free information flows is in this way reliant on the security provided by open peer review. This opens up such programmes to attacking programmers knowing exactly what they are facing, but at the same time it provides what is a cast-iron defence against claims of infiltration through embedded software, assuming that enough programmers have really examined the software.

Hacktivists have released a number of tools, some of which build on Tor and others which stand alone. Camera Shy is a system for hiding information within graphics embedded in web-pages. To use it someone encrypts information into a graphic, posts it on the web and then someone can decrypt the information using the Camera Shy browser and knowing the password (Camera Shy 2007). Scatterchat is an anonymous chat programme that builds on top of the Tor Network (Scatterchat 2007). And there are several other initiatives that, just as open source projects do, sometimes yield functioning and developing software programmes and sometimes do not.

The politics here is that of free flows of information and in that sense is distinct from mass action hacktivists who have their eyes firmly on other political issues, particularly those developing from the alter-globalisation movement. Information hacktivists most naturally connect to human rights and civil liberties activists within repressive regimes, as they try to determine technologies to support such activities.

Both information and mass action hacktivists face the difficulty, not unknown to non-virtual activists, that their politics is explicitly directed toward certain political goals but their techniques are in many ways modular and can be utilised by many different politics. Mass actions can be used by anyone, with the only limitation that they must legitimate their action by referring to the bodies who make it. A sense of democracy underlies mass action as its core political ethos. Information hacktivism similarly can be utilised by many, by anyone with the need for secure communication, with the defining ethos being that of ensuring free, secure access to information. A sense of information anarchism or libertarianism lies within information hacktivism.

Hacktivism pushes the revision of technology and society that hacking creates into some of the central political conflicts of the twenty-first century – the uneven effects of globalisation and the specificities of human rights. The nature of hacking may have been created in the deep nights of crackers worming their way into and through computer networks cross-pollinated with the long intensities of collective software coding released into the wilds of computer usage, but this nature has also run headlong, willfully, into grassroots conflicts over the nature of twenty-first-century societies.

Cyberwar: nation-states that hack

Estonia had been an early adopter of 'e-government', moving many government functions onto the Internet and, in the process, becoming more dependent on the Internet. Then, in late April and early May 2007, a range of odd and worrying things began to happen to Estonia's Internet. The websites of the Estonian presidency and parliament, of most government ministries, of political parties, of three of the six largest news organisations, of two of the biggest banks and a number of companies specialising in communications were all attacked simultaneously and repeatedly over several weeks, mainly using denial of service attacks that closed down the targeted websites. Blizzards of information destroyed Estonian connections to the Internet and rendered their services inaccessible. The culprit was largely thought to be, though they did not admit responsibility, the Russian government (Traynor 2007).

The attacks were linked to a complex dispute between Russia and Estonia. Following the collapse of the USSR and Estonia's independence from Russia, relations between the two nation-states had not been easy. There was a source of ongoing tension with Estonia housing many with ethnic

Russian backgrounds who had settled there when Estonia
had been absorbed into the USSR. Specific flashpoints also
emerged. For example, a plan to relocate a Soviet Second
World War memorial in April 2007 led to protests staged by
ethnic Russians, during which 1,300 people were arrested, 100
injured and one person killed. Russia's leader at the time,
Vladimir Putin, also made a number of speeches perceived as
being anti-Estonian (Traynor 2007). From 27 April, when
the memorial statue known as the Bronze Soldier was moved,
there suddenly appeared wide-ranging and well-targeted
denial of service attacks, which peaked on days associated with
some of Russia's most celebrated dates (Victory Day over Nazi
Germany, for example). Estonia responded by taking counter-
measures, many of which sought to isolate attacked sites from
the global Internet to ensure they were available for local
Estonian users. Subsequent analysis, unconfirmed, claimed
there was evidence that the attacker had hired extra 'bots' to
spew more information at Estonia, at one point creating 1 million attacking computers (Thomson 2007).

One difficulty with this story is knowing how much of it is
true. There is no doubt Estonia was massively attacked with its
political infrastructure well targeted but there is little way of
being sure that this was done as an official act of cyberwar by
the Russian government, however strongly circumstantial evidence suggests this was the case. Identification is a key issue
when cyberwar means Internet-based attacks by one nation-
state on another nation-state. There are a few other attacks that
are currently presumed to be an act of cyberwar between
nation-states, with two attacks on the USA and Europe being
candidates and coded by US authorities as Titan Rain and
Moonlight Maze.[2]

Titan Rain refers to a series of attacks since 2003 which
appear to be a co-ordinated attempt to gather information
about US and European government and military sites by
hackers based in China. Titan Rain is useful in demonstrating
some of the difficulties in identifying sources of cyberwar. The

SANS Institute concerns itself with exploring issues of security and cybersecurity and in 2005 its director Allan Paller claimed about Titan Rain attacks that 'These attacks come from someone with intense discipline. No other organization could do this if they were not a military organization. . . . [perpetrators] were in and out with no keystroke errors and left no fingerprints, and created a backdoor in less than 30 minutes. How can this be done by anyone other than a military organization?' (AFP 2005). Yet such attacks, with such precision, are documented in the non-military world of crackers. It is possible Paller was referring to a combination of precision and vast numbers of attacks, indicating some kind of disciplined organisation, yet even here crackers are known to have pulled off attacks of precision and extent. If this were all the evidence that existed then there could be no guarantee that this was a military attack.

Titan Rain also burst into the headlines in the UK, and Europe, in 2007 when reports appeared that hackers had broken into various UK government sites, both seeking classified information and forcing a crash of Parliament's Internet-based services. These attacks were linked to attacks on the USA, including what was reported to be the worst breach ever of the US military command at the Pentagon (the defence secretary's email system was thought to be compromised), and the Chinese military was accused of continuing the series of attacks that had been identified in 2003, though the evidence for the claim was not made public. Similar attacks on German government sites were tied into this pattern. There were reports of US and UK government officials complaining to the Chinese government about these attacks and links were made to the upcoming 17th Chinese Communist Party Congress, with one explanation suggesting the Chinese People's Liberation Army was using the cyberattacks for internal political manoeuvering. Within a few days, similar attacks on French government sites were also reported (Norton-Taylor 2007; Pilkington and Johnson 2007; Watts 2007).

Moonlight Maze is the designation for a series of intrusions into US government and military computers from 1999 which sought out and copied classified material. These attacks were traced to a computer physically located about 20 miles outside of Moscow. The attacks also appeared co-ordinated, in that they consistently sought out particular types of information. In what might be thought of as a minor detail but which may distinguish these attackers from crackers, it was recorded that attacks occurred roughly in Russian working hours and did not occur on Russian holidays (Drogin 1999). Such a working pattern is not typical of crackers but of employed crackers. Other rumoured incidents of cyberwar have occurred, with reports that the Pentagon considered and then rejected launching an all out cyberwar against Serbia during the Kosovo crisis. This attack included a reported plan to plunder Serbian leader Slobodan Milošović's bank accounts (Jordan and Taylor 2004: 28).

Cyberwar in the context of the wider nature of hacking can be taken to refer to cracks committed by nation-states. This has not always been the case, with cyberwar sometimes being taken to be any crack committed against a nation-state. However, it would be misleading to equate individual cracks or even intrusions by non-governmental groups with those committed by groups working officially at the direction of a nation-state's government. (In the next section, we will explore some of the reasons for this by distinguishing cyberterrorism from cyberwar.) Everard's analysis of the nature of the nation-state after the Internet's emergence explores many aspects of cyberwar and helps to identify the following definition of cyberwar as: information operations targeting computer-based distributed networks by a national-level adversary with computer-based means (Everard 2000: 103).

Cyberwar in this sense consists of crack-like attacks on the networked infrastructure of a nation-state by another nation-state. In the attack on Estonia, presumed to be sponsored by the Russian state, classic distributed denial of service (DDOS) techniques were used, including the use of 'zombies' or pro-grammes located on a wide range of computers around the Internet that on a command spew information directly to a target. Such ddos attacks are well known and documented as part of cracking and, as discussed in chapter 2, have produced a number of software packages to support them (Jordan and Taylor 2004: 75–6). In the example of Titan Rain, one nation-state employed techniques for infiltrating and accessing data held secret by another nation-state, again classic cracking activities.

This similarity with cracking poses a difficulty that Everard points out because it 'leads to . . . [a] blurred boundary, and one that poses perhaps the greatest difficulties for nation-states, and that is the boundary between warfare, criminal activity and plain old-fashioned system failure' (Everard 2000: 103). How are the representatives of a nation-state to know that a cyberattack is an act of warfare and not that of one or a few hackers? The case of British hacker Garry McKinnon is relevant here. Over several years ending in 2002, McKinnon illicitly accessed a wide range of US mili-tary, space research and other supposedly secure sites. Once tracked this would have looked very much like a series of co-ordinated intrusions because that is exactly what they were. McKinnon was, in his words, 'in search of suppressed technology, laughingly referred to as UFO technology. . . . Old-age pensioners can't pay their fuel bills, countries are invaded to award oil contracts to the West, and meanwhile secretive parts of the secret government are sitting on sup-pressed technology for free energy' (cited in Kelly 2006). His primary technique was to run an automated search for pass-words that was able to scan 65,000 machines in just over 8 minutes. This yielded high-level machines with administra-tor privileges, often with default passwords still set, and so allowed McKinnon to be able to do almost anything on those networks. Further techniques included, once when caught, telling the administrator who asked McKinnon who he was that he was from 'military computer security' and being believed.[3]

McKinnon's efforts were traced eventually to the one source, all data emanating from his computer also left a trail back to his computer, and he was arrested, leading to a long and controversial attempt by the US government to extradite him from the UK. The difference between McKinnon and the example known as Moonlight Maze is that once traced McKinnon was identified as an individual based in the UK whereas the Moonlight Maze attacks suggested a Russian base run by employees. But until the attacks are traced it would be difficult to know if these two examples represented intrusions organised by a nation-state or an individual.

The question of which actions constitute cyberwar also produces the blurred boundaries referred to by Everard. For example, the previous two examples might well be considered more as extensions of espionage than of war. There is obviously some truth to this point and the understanding of cyberwar offered here extends beyond a stereotyped, and now largely non-existent, vision of warfare between nation-states as open, bloody conflict between authorised personnel over territory. Not only is it questionable whether this vision existed and in which historical periods, but it has been permanently altered by the emergence of the Internet and the remote accessibility it offers. The reliance of the military, military research and essential parts of civilian infrastructure, such as power grids, dams and fuel supplies, on the Internet makes its use in warfare almost inevitable. Combined with hacking's revision of the separation and interaction between technologies and social structures, the concept of cyberwar becomes useful precisely because it tracks the opportunities for nation-states to attack other nation-states in varied and remote ways.

An alteration in the understanding of warfare has not just come from the Internet but is generally encapsulated under the heading a 'revolution in military affairs' (RMA) that takes account of a wide range of changes including increasing viability of unmanned craft, precision targeting systems such as cruise missiles, increased aids to individual soldiers such as global positioning and, of course, use of networked, computer-based communications. The RMA emerged from a series of military thinkers, some in the Soviet Union and then mainly in the West, who began to take seriously the possibility that this range of innovations meant that the nature of war and the military could be radically changed. Several armed forces (for example, the US and the Australian) commissioned studies on issues informing RMA, which then provided something close to blueprints for revised military structures. The extraordinarily one-sided victory of the USA in the first Gulf War was interpreted by many as the result of the technologies underlying RMA and gave extra legitimacy to its arguments (Everard 2000: 109–13).

RMA provides a wider context within which nation-states can integrate new techniques to provide new military forms. An example is the developing use of simulations in which the valuable resource of trained humans is kept away from bodily danger on a battlefield by utilising simulators which fly an actual machine. Though still futuristic, there are now complex forms of military simulation whose natural extension will be to utilise global networked communications to physically remove from battlefields the soldiers of technologically advanced countries who are still driving machines located on the battlefield (Der Derian 2001: 79–96). Der Derian argues this new military strategy relies on a military-industrial-media-entertainment (MIME) complex, of which the Internet is a key component.

The principles of hacking have been integrated into changes in warfare in a number of ways. Early on there were dire warnings of an 'Electronic Pearl Harbor' which some felt an unsecured US was facing. Such alarmism fed into changes such as the RMA or Derian's MIME. All these indicate that the revisions of technology and society pioneered in hacking have found uses in warfare. At the same time, the boundary blurring that Everard argues for and the focus on the Internet as part of warfare means that a notion of the 'military' clearly and absolutely distinct from civilian realms is almost impossible to maintain. One of the first documented acts undertaken by a nation-state in cyberspace was directed not at another nation-state but at a group of protesters. When the Electronic Disturbance Theater launched one of its mass hacktivist actions against the Pentagon, the US military launched a counter-strike seeking to prevent the electronic civil disobedience (Jordan and Taylor 2004: 90). We can now turn from nation-states to other actors who have taken up electronic arms.

Cyberterrorism

When the kinds of hacking techniques nation-states employ to conduct cyberwar are taken over by groups not in charge of a state, then we see the emergence of something called cyberterror. This topic has gained significant state and media attention since the (non-cyber) terrorist attacks on New York on September 11th and the subsequent 'war on terror'. The potential has been demonstrated by many crackers in their intrusions, from the closing down of sophisticated and well-funded e-commerce sites to the extensive explorations in search of 'free energy' by McKinnon. The possibility of cyberterror, as another limited and specific form of cracking, seems clear.

Despite what seems a clear possibility, cyberterror also suffers from some confusion because of the blurring of boundaries that we see with cyberwar; defining terrorism is even harder than defining war. The life of Nelson Mandela illustrates this with brutal clarity; he was called a terrorist and jailed as a terrorist for committing acts that seemed to be terrorist. Yet to many he was, even when jailed, a freedom fighter, and on being released became the first president of a non-apartheid South Africa, and latterly something close to a secular saint. In retrospect, many will consider the state that jailed

Mandela to be more terrorist than he was. Other related examples are Menachem Begin and Yitzhak Shamir, both of whom became prime minister of Israel after being part of terrorist groups during the struggle to form Israel. Both then dealt with violent opposition by demonising such opposition as terrorists (Whittaker 2001: 27). Terrorism requires considering the 'quality' or nature of the actions involved and is often a leaky concept drifting toward acts of war committed by nation-states or toward the actions of grassroots political groups. To see cyberterror, we need to examine the definition of terrorism a little more.

Yasser Arafat, then chairman of the Palestine Liberation Organisation, argued to the United Nations General Assembly in 1974 that: 'The difference between the revolutionary and the terrorist lies in the reason for which each fights. For whoever stands by a just cause and fights for the freedom and liberation of his land from the invaders, the settlers and the colonialists, cannot possibly be called a terrorist' (cited in Whittaker 2001: 6). Though Arafat's distinction may be a powerful rhetorical tactic and the examples of Mandela, Begin and Shamir suggest something similar, the opposition of terrorist and freedom fighter is a false one with each referring to a different phenomena. 'The notion of one man's terrorist is another man's freedom fighter is . . . a false dichotomy. You can be both. . . . The point is that one part of the terrorist-freedom fighter equation is a description of policy (terrorist/terrorism) while the other is a moral judgement on the nature of a belligerent (freedom fighter)' (Smith 1995: 232). As Smith points out, the equation of terrorist and freedom-fighter undermines an understanding of terrorism by transferring it into a moral realm, in which defining terrrorism is reduced to a political choice about which kinds of violence should be stigmatised. As nearly all governments and nearly all analysts accept the use of some violence as part of social policy (for example, we can think of the police), then terrorism's particular use of violence to provoke fear and uncertainty is not *a priori* morally repugnant (Smith 1995: 228–33). But, for our understanding of cyberterror, we can now see an alternative and helpful redefinition of terrorism as a policy.

While I cannot hope to create an entirely authoritative and final definition of terror, I can now suggest that a fruitful way forward is to see terror as a policy or strategy utilised by a range of actors. Within such a framework we can draw on both Whittaker's and Weimann's collations of other authors' definitions of terror from which a number of factors emerge to constitute an understanding of terror (Whittaker 1995: 3–5; Weimann 2006: 20–3). In both collections we find that the following elements are thought to constitute a terrorist act; premeditated, political, psychological and violent. Weimann notes arguments about a new form of terror emerging since September 11th and there are some divergences between Whittaker's and Weimann's surveys, yet the four factors are common. For present purposes we can now understand terrorism to mean the following. A terrorist act or terrorism is part of a premeditated planned strategy. Terrorism is a policy in the service of a political agenda, though what is meant by politics here should be taken broadly as including religious, ethnic, national and other politics. Terrorism aims at a psychological effect, so that its actions reverberate beyond their actual, material effects. Finally, terrorism involves violence beyond purely symbolic violence; it is not that terrorism does not involve symbolic violence but that such symbolic violence is attached to some form of material violence.

We should immediately note that there are some things that this definition rules out. First, the perpetrators of terrorism can be a range of actors, including state and non-state. Whether state-sponsored or state terrorism exists is a matter of policy choice by states, not analytic definition by theorists. Second, terrorism cannot be easily equated with guerrilla warfare, which may involve moments of terrorism but equally involves factors far more akin to war than to terror, such as geographically located boundaries. One can be a freedom-fighter and a terrorist, one can be in a nation-state's army and be a terrorist; terrorism is a strategy or policy which can be pursued by a range of agents.

It has been important to linger a few moments over the definition of terrorism in order to distinguish it from the grassroots politics of hacktivism and the nation-state conflicts of war, and it will become important to distinguish it from criminal activity, which will be discussed next. It is important also as terror has achieved a new centrality in global politics since September 11th, a point I can emphasise by noting that I write this paragraph on the day in 2007 in which a car bomb was driven into Glasgow airport and the day after two car bombs were found and defused in central London. The context of the 'war on terror' being fought by those who are defined by then US President George W. Bush as 'friends of freedom', is an emotionally charged context in which to consider the nature of cyberterror and so suggests the need for clarity.

In the context of hacking, the possibility of cyberterror seems all too obvious. The importance of the Internet and its vulnerability to revisions of technological determinism and social structures that hacking produces seems, as it was for both cyberwar and hacktivism, to produce a range of possibilities for terrorists. The understanding of terrorism so far developed is useful for we can rule out uses of the Internet prior to committing terrorist acts. In the wake of September 11th it was noted by the FBI's head of the US National Infrastructure Protection Center that the September 11th terrorists had 'used the net well' and, on one occasion, two of them had refused to check into a hotel until assured of round-the-clock Internet access in their room (Weimann 2006: 3). But in the present argument, using the Internet to communicate is not in itself a terrorist act even if the communication serves to enable terrorist acts. To get at the heart of cyberterror we need to put aside the communicative uses the Internet can be put to.

Our question must be, what acts of terror can be committed on the Internet? And there are a wide range of possibilities:

Terrorists, some argue, could . . . follow the hackers' lead and then, having broken into government and private computer systems, could cripple or at least disable the military, financial and service sectors of advanced economies. The growing dependence of our societies on information technology allows terrorists the chance to approach targets that would otherwise be utterly unassailable, such as national defence systems and air traffic control systems.

(Weimann 2006: 148)

Terrorists causing planes to fly into each other by infiltrating an air traffic control system, or taking over a dam and creating a flood, or remotely controlling military installations including missiles; all these have been floated as cyberterror possibilities. It was even claimed in the lead up to the second Iraq War that there was a thing called 'Iraq Net' which consisted of more than a hundred websites controlled by the Iraqi government of Saddam Hussein, which were just ready and waiting to launch denial of service attacks on the US information infrastructure. Like the famous weapons of mass destruction, however, Weimmann claimed as late as 2006 that no evidence had yet been found to confirm the existence of Iraq Net. From this and other examples Weimann argues that there are no confirmed cases of cyberterrorism (Weimann 2006: 150, 14).

The lack of confirmed attacks does not mean the threat is non-existent and some countries have explored what a cyberterror threat might mean. The US has led the way in simulations of possible terror attacks. In 1997 the US National Security Agency commissioned 35 teams of official crackers to attempt to infiltrate US Pentagon systems using only tools found on the Internet. Using tools easily downloaded, such as brute force password crackers (that is, programmes that automatically and quickly try possible passwords) and social engineering, they gained access to dozens of critical Pentagon systems (Verton 2003: 31–52). This simulation suggested that not only Pentagon systems but, in particular, energy systems, were vulnerable to being cracked. Though the result of this and other incidents was that information security moved rapidly up many organisations' agendas, it should be remembered that cracks continue using many similar techniques. In 2005, the CIA simulated a wide-ranging attack, using the codename Silent Horizon, to test the capability of US institutions to react. Though no real probing of systems was undertaken, this exercise further established the real concern of cyberterrorism for some nation-states (Weimann 2006: 168–9).

Yet, even given such concerns, it remains the case that very few actual examples of cyberterrorism exist, far fewer than cyberwar, hacktivism or, as we shall see, cybercrime. There remains the possibility of terrorists pressing hacking's technological determinations of information technology and networks into service but there are few confirmed examples. Verton's 2003 study is littered with examples of possible plots, few of which were enacted. Verton's evidence is almost entirely derived from government contacts who are almost always anonymous, meaning his evidence cannot be corroborated against known incidents (Verton 2003). This does not mean that we should dismiss Verton's work but it does mean that Weimann's later survey and the nature of Verton's evidence, creates a significant doubt about the existence of cyberterrorist incidents. Weimann's 2006 published survey argues:

> Amid all the dire warnings and alarming statistics that the subject of cyberterrorism generates, it is important to remember one simple statistic: so far, there has been no recorded instance of a terrorist cyberattack on US public facilities, transportation systems, nuclear power plants, power grids, or other key components of the national infrastructure.
> (Weimann 2006: 164)

In Japan in 2000 the Metropolitan Police Department reported that a software system which tracked locations of police vehicles had been developed by members of the Aum Shinryko cult, which in 1995 killed 12 people in a gas attack on a subway. It turned out cult members had also developed software for 80 Japanese companies and 10 other government agencies. Cybersecurity expert Professor Dorothy Denning noted that the cult could have installed easy access for itself or tools for launching attacks (Denning 2001). Unfortunately for those looking for a live example of a real cyberterror attack, Denning was only pointing at possibilities and not real actions. Weimann also mentions the example of a disgruntled worker in Australia attempting to discharge a million gallons of raw sewage as an example of a possible type of terror attack, but this example was related to work issues rather than terror. Weimann and Verton also note recent examples of al Qaeda recruits being sent on training to learn encryption and breaking encryption (Weimann 2006: 167, 170; Verton 2003: 124).

It is clear many of the specific tools and techniques of cracking would be available to terrorists and if applied to our growing reliance on the Internet and computer networks, a potential risk appears. This risk is the application of hacking's ability to redraw technological determinism in the virtual, supplying new and far-reaching powers to those who redesign technologies to create new opportunities for social action. That such actions could aim to terrorise by causing violence for political gain is clearly possible. However, given that no or very few such attacks have actually been recorded and that this lack of attacks should be viewed in the light of the many instances of cracking, hacktivism, some cyberwar actions and many cybercrimes, we can conclude this section by noting we are dealing in cyberterror with possibilities rather than realities. This is not so for our next section on cybercrime.

Cybercrime

In 2006 José Manuel García Rodríguez, who in Argentina went by the unflattering nickname 'the fat Spaniard' but was known online as the hacker 'Tasmania', was arrested in Buenos Aires and deported to Spain accused of stealing 'thousands of Euros' by cracking. Rodríguez was accused of 'stealing passwords to bank accounts' and of using them to extract significant amounts of money (Eazel 2006).

In 2006–7 an estimated £600,000 was stolen from accounts at the Swedish bank Nordea. Someone had sent fake emails to customers with a trojan horse programme attached which installed itself on a customer's computer and recorded their keystrokes, in this way recording their log-in details. This information was routed first to US-based servers and then passed automatically onto Russian servers, where it was used to siphon funds from users' accounts (Out-Law News 2007).

In 2007 the fashion world thrilled to the divorce case between multimillionaire founder of the Jimmy Choo shoe empire Tamara Mellon and her then husband, multimillionaire Mathew Mellon. During the case Mathew Mellon was accused of hiring a detective agency to crack his wife's computers. The London-based detective agency Active Investigation Services was said to have sent emails to Tamara Mellon that purported to have confidential information about Mathew Mellon that would help her divorce case, but were actually trojan horse viruses that would have installed themselves and recorded all her keystrokes, sending them back to the detective agency. During the trial, the detective agency was accused of using the same tactics in a series of other cases, as well as breaking into telephone equipment to set up phone bugs (Taylor 2007).

In 1996, some Russian crackers developed ways of illicitly entering Citibank systems. They did this for classic cracking reasons of exploration and showed no interest in moving money illicitly. However, one of the crackers was contacted by criminals and was eventually persuaded (the cracker claimed it was when he was drunk and depressed) to explain how to access Citibank for the reward of US$100 and two bottles of vodka. The criminals then organised a raid that it is claimed netted as much as US$10 million (Gow and Norton-Taylor 1996).

Bank accounts broken into and money transferred and illicit surveillance installed on target computers to aid a more favourable divorce settlement are types of cybercrime. The bank hacks, so clearly crimes with their implication of virtual John Dillingers sticking up banks, also break into two types. The Citibank raid conjures up visions of being able to remotely transfer funds, sitting safely at a distance, whereas the Nordea raid relied on tricking individuals and then automating the harvesting of information from them, more like illicitly memorising someone's computer card code as it is used in an automated teller. Clearly, we seem to have here a number of examples of crime committed over the Internet. Wall's work on these phenomena suggests that:

> Whatever its merits and demerits, the term 'cybercrime' has now entered the public parlance and we are now stuck with it. The term has greater meaning if it is understood in terms of the mediation of criminal or harmful behaviour by networked technology . . . If the hallmark of cyberspace is that it is informational, networked and global, then these qualities should also be characteristic of cybercrime.
>
> (Wall 2007: 208)

To understand cybercrime we can look at Wall's definition of types of cybercrime. For simplicity I will take his four-part definition, particularly because it is a categorisation that was broadly endorsed by Yar's work (Yar 2006; Wall 2001, 2007). Wall argued that there were four types of cybercrime. Cybertrespass which involves crossing boundaries into other people's property, such as cracking or defacing websites. Cybertheft which involves stealing other people's property, for example by illicitly gaining their credit card details and using them. Cyberpornography which involves breaking laws on obscenity. And, cyberviolence is doing psychological harm and/or inciting physical harm against others, for example by being abusive in online fora (Wall 2001: 3–7; Yar 2006: 9–11).

In all cases, we come across familiar techniques from hacking. Breaking into targeted computers is part of all the examples given and it utilises cracking techniques of either harvesting or cracking passwords, exploiting known vulnerabilities and so on. In the 1996 attack on Citibank, we even see how it was crackers with no interest in personal gain who created the ability to transfer money illicitly but it was cybercriminals who utilised the method. As with cyberterror and cyberwar, we find the elements of cracking all present and correct.

It might be thought that the Free Software/Open Source component of hacking is harder to find in cybercrime, and it is perhaps so in the examples given so far. But if we take up Wall's cybertheft category we are led to consider piracy on the Internet. This is the ability to download goods that can be digitised, such as music or movies, that are also under copyright. Because they can be digitised such goods can be downloaded across the Internet and the emergence of peer-to-peer systems makes such piracy potentially widespread. It is Open Source techniques of software production that largely fuel such peer-to-peer (p2p) networks. Peer-to-peer networks swap files by connecting all those who wish to download or upload a file together as peers. Most computer networks consist of computers operating at any one time as a server (providing files) or a client (receiving requested files); peer-to-peer innovates by making all connected computers simultaneously servers and clients. This means that when someone connects they may begin to download a file but at the same time the files they have available and those they download will be registered and will be available to others for upload.

For a peer-to-peer network to exist someone has to write code, debug it and distribute it, usually gaining some help along the way. This code has to provide some kind of organisation to the network, some communication forms which mark files and locate them so that others can find them and some forms of client that can be used by anybody who can use a point-and-click-based computer. For example, a network such as Bit Torrent creates a 'torrent' file for every download and these torrents can then be published. This torrent then connects to trackers (which may be centralised or may themselves be distributed among peers) that keep track of who has the files and so directs connections between peers. Peers then download small sections of the targeted file, allowing many peers to upload and download the same file at the same time. Downloading a torrent file usually means a slow-starting download which gradually increases in speed as more peers are located and connected, this is in distinction to single-site downloads where the top speed is usually established quickly. Bit Torrent is supported by a number of clients, many of which are licensed and developed as open source and the core protocols that define bit torrent are released under a variant of the GNU Public Licence.

The point about piracy is that anything that can be digitised can be a file and can be traded using such networks as peer-to-peer. The music industry has been particularly vociferous in attacking the trading of files as piracy and theft, but the point holds for movies, television shows, software and any other digitised file that has been copyrighted. Again, we see the techniques of hacking applied for certain purposes that are not strictly speaking at the core of hacking's concerns.

Though we have more recorded instances of cybercrime than cyberterror or cyberwar, this does not mean cybercrime is soberly discussed, and free of sensationalism. Instead, as with many phenomena associated with the Internet, the opposite is the case. In the examples used to begin this discussion of cybercrime we can see this at work. The case of the Fat Spaniard was reported widely across Internet-based news sites but nearly all used exactly the same report, most likely deriving from a news agency. This report does not specify how Rodríguez performed his crimes, has no solid information about how much he may have stolen and focuses on the more sensational aspects of his case (in this case his possible jail term of 40 years, his international extradition and his strange nickname). The case of Nordea was reported mainly from a statement issued by McAfee, an Internet security company. The statement is notable for emphasising that customers who had money stolen were all lacking anti-virus protection, which is one of McAfee's main products.

When considering other cybercrimes, particularly pae-dophilia both in the online provision of images and cases of grooming and cyberstalking of children, there is also consider-able attention, that at times seems out of proportion to the number of crimes being considered. Yar feels compelled to consider whether issues of online paedophilia are more like a moral panic than a reflection of real or even potential abuse (Yar 2006: 133–6).

Cybercrimes utilise hacking techniques but in the service of personal gain. The types of gain are no different to other crimes, be they monetary, informational, sexual or some other. I need to emphasise motivations and what is gained by the criminal because it is not always easy to distinguish much cracking from cybercrime on the basis of actions taken. We have an example of this in the case of the Citibank hack where the action taken differs between crackers and cybercriminals and not in the fact that laws were broken; both illegally entered Citibank's computers, but cybercriminals used the techniques for personal monetary gain and crackers maintained a differ-ent interest in exploration.

This distinction is important to note, in concluding on cybercrime, for two reasons. First, many of the early studies of cybercrime focused on cracking even where the crackers involved showed no demonstrable gain other than intellectual challenges. This does not make what crackers do 'not crime' but it does make it into a peculiar and specific form of crime. Both the Wall and Thomas and Loader collections from early 2000 integrate discussion of cracking within cybercrime. It is only with later discussions, such as those in Yar's and Wall's later book, that this distinction is better recognised (Thomas and Loader 2001; Yar 2006; Wall 2001, 2007). Second, crack-ers themselves often blur the distinction, sometimes develop-ing a kind of second-order criminality which is used to support their first-order desire for exploration and control of computer networks. The cost of equipment or phone charges which might have prevented cracking has at times been met by using stolen credit card details, with the justification of such monetary gain being that it is in the service of cracking's ideals or compulsions.

Cybercrime is with us and requires increasing defences. Like hacktivism, it is a more substantial and better-documented phenomenon than cyberwar or cyberterror. However, like all three other phenomena so far discussed in this chapter we see the utilisation of hacking techniques in ways that extend hacking beyond its core.

Hacking the social

The distinction between using hacking techniques and being at the core of hacking is a fine one. This leads to the boundaries I have drawn in this chapter often being blurred. Not only are there individuals who will move across these categories but the distinctions are themselves already slender. If we were to focus narrowly and exclusively on the actions of hacktivists, cyberwarriors, cyberterrorists and cybercriminals then we would have a difficult time seeing a distinction between them and those at the centre of hacking.

Motivation is a useful discriminator to begin with. Hacktivists aim at political change. Cyberwarriors engage in inter-nation-state conflict to further their own nation-state's interests. Cyberterrorists look for political effects by inflicting psychologically resonant violence. Cybercriminals seek personal gain. These four motivations distinguish hacking the social from hacking. Yet motivation may also be a weak discriminator because it relies on an understanding of the intentions of actors. Not only is it often difficult to access such intentions, it also remains unclear whether someone's claimed intentions are their real intentions, particularly when dealing with the kind of phenomena this chapter explores.

Motivations are useful but they become acutely useful if we recognise that they derive from a more significant distinction between those who hack the social and those who hack. All four categories explored in this chapter are groups that seek social change. Whether it is the explicit political demands of hacktivists or terrorists, or the aspirations of a nation-state's representatives, or even the micro-concerns of cybercriminals to utilise changed social conditions for personal gain; all four intervene in the social. All four groups hack for social change, but hackers see hacking as social change.

Hackers redraw the boundaries of social and technological determinations, making them both fluid and compelling, exploding our previous ways of inter-relating between 'social' forces and 'technological' forces, while at the same time incorporating and recreating our understanding of the ways technological and social determinations occur. Hackers in these processes are hacking and making social changes simultaneously, one in and of the other. The four groups this chapter has explored all take hold of these changes and then apply them to aspects of the social. Though closely related to hacking, hacktivists, cyberwarriors, cyberterrorists and cybercriminals are not mainly hackers but are, at their core, users of hacking.

Notes

1 This poster also claimed that the 9/11 attack was a Bush family operation involving a controlled demolition of the Twin Towers and called for the uncovering of the conspiracy, perhaps meaning we might expect his claims to have less validity than other more technical interventions.

2 Wikipedia has a useful summary of relevant newspaper articles and reports on Titan Rain and Moonlight Maze. See http://en.wikipedia.org/wiki/Titan_Rain and http://en.wikipedia.org/wiki/Moonlight_Maze.

3 Again, Wikipedia has a useful summary of relevant material on Gary McKinnon. See http://en.wikipedia.org/wiki/Gary_Mc Kinnon

Hacking the Non-Hack: Creative Commons, Hackers who don't Programme, Programming Proletariat, Hacking Sub-Cultures and Nerds and Geeks

Programming and hacking

All diverse communities extend themselves in creative and sometimes odd ways. People take action and invent new types of actions; in these processes they may begin from existing communities, while also creating hybrid communities which offer new social forms. Hacking is no exception, with the implications of some of its innovations being extended outside the world of computers and networks and its culture gaining wider acceptance with those who could in very few senses of the term be called hackers. In particular, the activity of programming is so integral to hacking that it is not often separated out. Exploring this separation of programming from hacking will allow further complexities of hacking to be examined. This chapter will continue filling out the full meaning of hacking by outlining a succession of hackers who do not hack, whether they programme or not – hackers of the non-hack.

There are four distinct groups here. First, there are those who have taken up Free Software's innovations around copyright and look to extend this politics of distribution more generally. Second, there are those who play interesting roles within hacking but who do not themselves engage with programming; publishers, conference organisers and publicists have been important to hacking but do they hack? Third, there are those who programme but who have the ability of hackers to intervene in socio-technological determinations stripped away, and in compensation are offered salaries and hacking cultures. The programming proletariat code away in digital factories at the dictates at the market and they may dress like hackers but they are non-hackers. Finally, there are sub-cultures of hacking with distinct groups devoted to specific pursuits; here we meet cypherpunks, virus writers and hardware hackers. Looking at sub-cultures also allows us to see a purely symbolic version of hacking in the figures of the nerd and the geek. We can look at these in turn.

Property and the Commons: free, not as in free beer but as in free culture

> As hacks go, the GPL stands as one of Stallman's best. It created a system of communal ownership within the normally proprietary confines of copyright law. More importantly, it demonstrated the intellectual similarity between legal code and software code. Implicitly within the GPL's preamble was a profound message: instead of viewing copyright law with suspicion, hackers should view it as yet another copyright system begging to be hacked.
>
> (Williams 2002: 127)

As already discussed, the GPL and more general notions of copyleft do not attack or undermine existing notions of property. Instead they try to utilise existing legal notions of property to create counter-intuitive results. Instead of laws that lock property down and exclude users, GPL-like licences require everyone who uses a particular property to share it and, moreover, to share any improvements. This relies on the digital nature of software, a commodity that can be used simultaneously by many people and for which there are effectively no restrictions on how many of each commodity there can be.

The creation of a hack-inspired non-hack related to copyleft is based on the idea that the strategy the GPL and like licences develop for software should be extended to other copyrights, particularly to copyrights related to culture and ideas. Stallman's defence of digital rights to access, improve and share software could similarly allow access to things like books, audiovisual items, music and so on. While slogans such as 'free culture' have been used in this context, it is probably most accurate to think in terms of 'free digital information', if we take information in a broad sense that includes information conveyed by images, sound and the inter-relations between these. We should also note that information may be embodied in different ways, for example movies may exist as a file on the Internet, as DVDs to be played or as high production versions only to be used in theatres. Similarly, information may be embodied in drugs or other material forms. This distinction becomes important as it is not the material vehicle through which information is delivered that is centrally at stake in these ideas but the information itself.

For example, Wikipedia is an online encyclopaedia, with millions of entries on all manner of subjects. Anyone who wishes can start a topic or contribute to an existing topic. By clicking on parts of the Wikipedia website one is taken to pages which allow alterations or the addition of new material. Wikipedia is then not just an encyclopaedia but a collaborative encyclopaedia which can expand and become as accurate (or inaccurate) as its contributors allow. In mid 2007 there were, according to Wikipedia, 75,000 active contributors working on 5.3 million articles in more than 100 languages, with just over 1.8 million articles in English. This leads to some interesting effects. In a normal encyclopaedia the most recent editions and articles would usually be expected to be the most accurate, because they would have drawn on the most recent information. This is the opposite for Wikipedia, because the longer an article has been on Wikipedia the more people are likely to have worked on it, spotted mistakes or vandalism and produced a more accurate article. Those using Wikipedia are even advised to be cautious when using recently added or edited material and to consider it with suspicion.

Wikipedia itself runs on the open source software programme MediaWiki. However, for the purposes of free culture the important point is that information posted on Wikipedia is subject to the GNU Free Documentation Licence (GFDL). GFDL was initially designed for manuals or documentation that supported software released under GPL and it allows the copying and modification of documents as long as modifications are also released under GFDL. There is controversy about GFDL, which has some technical difficulties whose details are not essential here, but the point to note is the extension of Stallman's original creative appropriation of copyright law in regard to software to a website that relies primarily on text.

The lack of authoritative fact checking before articles go live on Wikipedia has been questioned. However, in a sign of the potential strength of open source information creation beyond software, a study found that deliberate slanders or misinformation posted on Wikipedia were 'rapidly and effectively' repaired by the Wikipedia community and that 'one type of malicious edit we examined is typically repaired within two minutes' (Viegas *et al*. 2004: 575–6). Wikipedia demonstrates the potential for hacking information beyond software and some have identified a political, or community, need for such a hack.

These kinds of arguments are most closely associated with Lawrence Lessig and his founding of the Creative Commons, though more recently Benkler's arguments about the shift within information economies to networked information economies have also contributed (Benkler 2006). Lessig takes up Stallman's starting point, which at heart asserts that property is good not bad. 'A culture without property, or in which creators can't get paid, is anarchy, not freedom. Anarchy is not what I advance here' (Lessig 2004: xvi). However, property can also be used to unreasonably restrict access to ideas, in ways that are socially detrimental. Lessig's argument is that we face just such a time at the beginning of the twenty-first century. An example of Lessig's argument is his exploration of the release of cheap 'generic' drugs to help Aids treatment in Africa. He notes that the US government in the late 1990s stepped in to oppose a law passed in South Africa that would have allowed cheaper drugs to be imported but, it was argued, this would have transgressed international agreements on patent law. There was no question of direct economic loss here, keeping the drugs at high prices by protecting patents meant simply that most Africans would not have been able to buy the drugs at all.

> Now let's step back for a moment. There will be a time thirty years from now when our children look back at us and ask, how could we have let this happen? How could we allow a policy to be pursued whose direct cost would be to speed the death of 15 to 30 million Africans, and whose only real benefit would be to uphold the 'sanctity' of an idea?
>
> (Lessig 2004: 260)

Lessig here provides an example which demonstrates that if, in his eyes, a lack of property is unacceptable because it leads to a lack of freedom and to anarchy, then at the same time an over-emphasis on property rights can strangle cultures and kill people. Lessig outlines a situation in which government officials are not only interpreting intellectual property as something to be protected but also perceive a need to prevent anyone voluntarily waiving such rights or to redefine property as anything but exclusion. This justification was used to prevent a scheduled discussion within the World Intellectual Property Organization (WIPO) in 2003 about open source software, because FOSS encouraged the waiving of copyright (Lessig 2004: 262–9). Lessig argues that such a view implies a particular property system.

> There is a history of just such a property system that is well known in the Anglo-American tradition. It is called 'feudalism'. Under feudalism, not only was property held by a relatively small number of individuals and entities. And not only were the rights that ran with that property powerful and extensive. But the feudal system had a strong interest in

assuring that property holders within that system not weaken feudalism by liberating people or property within their control to the free market.

(Lessig 2004: 267)

Lessig's argument is that a middle way on property is needed between anarchy and feudalism; a middle way that weighs social benefits of access to ideas alongside an individual creator's rights to remuneration. Further, he argues that under the cloak of protecting the creator highly restrictive laws and uses of copyright and patents are being implemented; uses which are not conducive to creative cultures or to humane care. From such arguments Lessig founded the Creative Commons (http://creativecommons.org/). It is not so much a question here of whether Lessig's arguments are correct or not, judging such a thing would take far longer than is appropriate when sketching in the issues of hacking copyright, but it is important to see that such arguments were strong enough to underpin the creation of the Creative Commons, which embodies a hacking non-hack.

There are also other ways than through Lessig's work to reach such a position. We could approach similar arguments by examining Benkler's claims about the way computer networks have revolutionised information economies creating, Benkler argues, opportunities for cultures and economies to develop rapidly and in more egalitarian ways but which existing and entrenched interests are going to oppose and try to stifle. In the new networked economy, as Benkler defines it, those such as the recording industry are likely to try and hold back innovations that threaten their existing institutional structures. Opposing such interests leads to many similar positions between Benkler and Lessig, particularly regarding the importance of extending FOSS notions of copyright (Benkler 2004).

It is primarily, though not solely, through Creative Commons that Stallman's initial insight into inverting copyright law has been extended beyond software. Of course, the initial move is made in the GFDL which relates to text and which grew out of support for GPLd software, but it is in Creative Commons that the need for a wide range of licences which deal with the different issues that arise from different creative products is met. Creative Commons supports a wide range of activities, educational, promotional, political lobbying and so on, that encourage support for Lessig's middle way on copyright. At the heart of this work is the provision of a range of different licences which meet the needs of authors.

Creative Commons defines an array of different licences and supports, each with legal code (which satisfies existing legal structures and makes the licence binding), a 'creative commons deed' (which states in plain language what the licence allows and disallows), and with symbols like the well-known copyright (©) that can be stamped on the object being licensed. A basic licence requires attribution, just the demand that people retain the author's credit on the object but can use the object in all other ways. From here there are licences which add the requirement that any remix or reuse of an object be released with the same licence, licences which allow or disallow commercial uses of an object, and so on (see http://creative commons.org/about/licenses/meet-the-licenses).

Creative Commons is an institutionalised hack of copyright. It reworks the hacker tactic of copyleft in a different environment. However, the inclusion of a licence which restricts changing the creative object marks Creative Commons as dealing with something that differs from software. We can remember that the ability to change software was at the heart of Stallman's ideals and Free Software/Open Source projects. Yet Creative Commons explicitly creates licences which prevent such rewriting of a creative object. Creative Commons has to deal with information objects, such as creative writing, music or pictures, which the individual creator may not wish people to be able to change. Within Free Software the whole point is to open out code to many eyeballs and to utilise the strength of a community to improve the object. But this is not always the case when one or a few people collaborate to produce what they consider a finished object, finished not because it could not be different but because as an artistic product the object is finished because its creators have achieved the effects or sensibility they wished for.

Here the importance of the object to hacking takes centre stage. It is the nature of the different informational or creative objects at stake which differentiate efforts on copyright such as the Creative Commons from those found in Free Software/Open Source. The object of hacking is, in the nature of software code, both creative, malleable and amenable to collective intervention. Moreover, the test of its utility is primarily whether 'it runs' and only secondarily are there choices between code based on aesthetic markers such as elegance or conformity to Unix cultures of simplicity. When dealing with a wider range of artistic products this test of the creative object no longer applies. The question for a piece of music or prose of whether 'it runs' is far more complex and does not have the ability software has to reach closure through a technological moment. For example, does a word processing programme provide cut and paste options and do they work? It is clear how the test 'does it run' can apply to such a question. But, 'is a piece of music danceable?' or 'is a poem beautiful?' are not amenable to a similar test. Rather, the artist who produces such objects may wish to ensure their creation stays as created because there is no way of defining 'better'. We are dealing with an entirely different set of creative products in music, prose, poetry, film and so on than we are dealing with in software. We have moved outside of hacking because the informational objects and the ways of determining what are good and bad objects have shifted fundamentally.

These distinctions mark the work of Lessig and many others on copyright as being outside hacking, though of course closely related. These are people hacking a non-hack. They have taken a tactic, an idea of hacking, and noticed it has wider application than to computers and networks. This application itself has wide social ramifications touching on some central issues of information societies, such as piracy and creative rights, but it has extended beyond hacking while remaining inspired by hacking.

Non-programmers hacking

As well as lawyers and artists who have taken hacking outside to the non-hack, there are many lawyers who have contributed to hacking within hacking. We have discussed the GNU Public License (GPL) without going into detail but it is worth mentioning that there have been three versions of the GPL, with the most recent released in June 2007 after two years' public consultation. GPL v.3 (as the GNU Public Licence version 3 is called in shorthand) was written by Richard Stallman, who had been primarily responsible for v.1 and v.2, and Eben Moglen, professor of law and legal history at Columbia University and founder of the Software Freedom Law Centre (http://www.software freedom.org/). Though computer programming literate, before becoming a lawyer Moglen was involved in designing computer languages; Moglen's contribution to a central component of hacking in the GPL is as a lawyer. If we think of Lessig as a lawyer who took a principle of hacking outside of the hack – hacking a non-hack – then we can think of Moglen as a non-programmer working in hacking. To further understand the nature of hacking, it is worth exploring how non-programmers may become hackers, in distinction to non-programmers who take hacking ideas outside of hacking. We can look briefly at two examples in a lawyer and a strategist/publicist.

Eben Moglen was drawn into hacking after beginning as a computer programmer then leaving to do a history and then law degree. As a lawyer he came back to hacking first by offering legal services to Phil Zimmerman, who was at that time being prosecuted by the US government for offering free strong encryption, and then working with Stallman. Moglen's motivation comes out in something he wrote to Stallman: 'I wrote him an email in which I said I use EMACS every day; it'll be a long time before you exhaust your entitlement to free legal help from me' (cited in Moody 2006). As Moglen's commitment grew he decided to set up an institutional infrastructure in the Software Freedom Law Centre. This is a legal advice centre set up as a charity to offer legal services and representation to support free and open source software. The Centre was set up in 2005 with US$4 million donated by the Open Source Development Labs which was in turn funded by a number of corporations to promote Open Source development (including Fujitsu, IBM, Hewlett-Packard and others). I will touch briefly on GPL v.3 to demonstrate the importance of this non-programming to hacking.

We have looked at Stallman's fundamental idea which fuels the GPL that ideas around property can be inverted to protect distribution and access rather than to restrict access. But such an idea needs to work in a range of legal contexts for it to have worth. If someone were to take a Free or Open Source programme, modify it and refuse to distribute the modifications, thereby denying the basis of the whole movement, then what would happen? Community pressure is one answer. Those who did such a thing would most likely lose the support of the FOSS community and the programming power that comes with it. But a second, important, answer is litigation. If the original software had been licensed using GPL or another similar licence then modifying the software and refusing to release those modifications in source code should be illegal. The perpetrator could then be taken to court, just as anyone who transgresses a copyright can be taken to court. But this, in turn, requires confidence that the licence is legally binding.

As noted in chapter 3 early licences were simplistic, such as the already quoted trn licence:

> Copyright © 1985, Larry Wall
> You may copy the trn kit in whole or in part as long as you don't try to make money off it, or pretend that you wrote it.
> (Cited in Williams 2002: 125)

More developed licences provide both legal security and community acceptance: the legal licence has to put into practice a particular ethical view of software and its production and so the technical legal language must also gain acceptance as a true or good version of the community's vision. For example, I have several times discussed the basic idea of stating that modifications to GPLd software must themselves be released under the same licence but to establish this legally specific forms of language must be used. Here are some of the preliminary definitions from GPL v.3:

> To 'modify' a work means to copy from or adapt all or part of the work in a fashion requiring copyright permission, other than the making of an exact copy. The resulting work is called a 'modified version' of the earlier work or a work 'based on' the earlier work.

> To 'propagate' a work means to do anything with it that, without permission, would make you directly or secondarily liable for infringement under applicable copyright law, except executing it on a computer or modifying a private copy. Propagation includes copying, distribution (with or without modification), making available to the public, and in some countries other activities as well.

> (GPL v.3 2007)

These are not substantive sections but merely the 'boilerplate', the basic definitions which will then be woven into a licence. The core of the GPL comes after a series of such basic definitions and is stated in similar legal terminology. I have quoted them to demonstrate the kind of technical language that is needed. Not only must such language be generated but it must be checked to ensure it is strong enough and it must be discussed with the Free Software and Open Source community to ensure it embodies their ethics. The first underlines the importance of legal expertise in this context, while the second emphasises different skills. To ensure the community had a chance to express its views about GPL v.3, Moglen and Stallman produced a draft which was then subject to two years' discussion, and two further substantial redrafts. One example of the difficulty of this process is that Torvalds was, and in mid-2007 remained, negative about moving the Linux kernel from GPL v.2 to v.3, though he has also suggested there may be some benefits (Torvalds 2007).

Given the huge importance of licences to Free Software and Open Source programmes, Moglen's work demonstrates that hacking contains non-programmers. Moglen also demonstrates both the need for specific expertise in his legal work and the need for other more general skills such as organisational, as shown by the importance of a consultation process. A second example of a non-programming hacker has already been mentioned in chapter 3 in the figure of strategist/publicist Erik Raymond.

Raymond was a programmer, having overseen a number of programming efforts, the most notable of which was probably the fetchmail email client. However, he also demonstrated an interest in public presentation of Free Software, particularly after he became aware of the organisation or dis-organisation of the Linux community. He first tried out a Linux-style development on a software project, but even more importantly he wrote up the lessons he learned from that project in his widely influential (already discussed in chapter 3) essay 'The Cathedral and the Bazaar'. Raymond's very strong conviction was, that software produced according to the principles of Free Software was superior and produced a better working method for both creating and improving software. However, he was also of the strong opinion that the rhetoric around freedom that had, for years, been produced by Richard Stallman and the Free Software Foundation, was holding back acceptance of this software and its underlying methods. Raymond argued:

> The real disagreement between OSI [Open Source Initiative] and FSF [Free Software Foundation], the real axis of discord between those who speak of 'open source' and 'free software', is not over principles. It's over tactics and rhetoric. The open-source movement is largely composed not of people who reject RMS's [Richard Stallman] ideals, but rather of people

who reject his *rhetoric*. . . . So when RMS insists that we talk about 'computer users' rights', he's issuing a dangerously attractive invitation to us to repeat old failures. It's one we should reject – not because his principles are wrong, but because that kind of language, applied to software, simply does not persuade anybody but us. In fact, it confuses and repels most people outside our culture.

(Raymond 1999)

Raymond took this stance, and the publicity associated with his Cathedral/Bazaar essay, and utilised his skills in speaking, writing and organising to create both a new name for Free Software as well as organisations and ideas to drive the new name home. Raymond had some help, from, for example Tim O'Reilly the publisher, who also felt that the aggressive rhetoric that Stallman favoured, which explicitly and repeatedly pushed forward the importance of freedom, needed to be moved to the background. Once in the background, but not absent, the advantages of software produced according to free software principles could expand and grow thereby also promoting substantially but not explicitly its values of freedom. In particular, they hoped that some businesses would join in, adding financial and programming muscle to the movement. An example of this process is the naming of whatever free software is when it is not called Free Software, Raymond argued that calling it 'free' emphasised exactly what he felt needed to be underplayed.

This discussion progressed through a number of conferences and meetings, drawing in a range of Free Software programmers of note as well as those such as Raymond and O'Reilly whose input to FOSS was primarily not through programming. The key problem was the confusion in English between free as 'no cost' and free as 'freedom'. Though Stallman had always emphasised the latter, the very term was felt to indicate free as in no payment, which was scaring companies otherwise interested in Free Software. Torvalds, who at this time had just moved to California, even commented at one stage in the debate that he had only just learned there was a difference in English between free as 'libre' and free as 'gratis' (Williams 2002: 164). Into this mixture came the decision of Netscape, then the owner and producer of one of the two most popular web browsers as well as popular server software, to move its code to a Free Software licence. Netscape's decision is complex and draws on many factors, not least a need to deal with a declining if not failing market position, but for present purposes we can simply note that here seemed to be the opportunity Raymond and others were hoping for to bring commercial corporations into Free Software (Moody 2001: 166–7). In February 1998, Raymond convened a meeting at a GNU/Linux hardware company of around six people, not including Stallman, and at this meeting the name Open Source was suggested (Moody 2001: 167; Williams 2002: 161–2).

Soon after a conference on Freeware drew together many of those active in Free Software but did not include an invitation to Stallman (though Raymond claims he argued Stallman should be included) and the need for a new name was discussed. A range of names were suggested at a sesssion at the conference, such as freeware, sourceware and freed software, and a vote was taken that Open Source won, though not uninamiously (Moody 2001: 167; Williams 2002: 163–5). Raymond, O'Reilly and others concerned with promoting the movement then moved to promote the new term. The Open Source Initiative, an institution to promote Open Source software, was created and a definition of Open Source written. The initiative has been successful in that Open Source has become a widely known term for Free Software, such that now many refer to Free and Open Source Software (FOSS) or often simply to Open Source. Stallman refused (and in late 2007 still refuses) to engage with the term, arguing that freedom *is* the point and that he is only involved with Free Software which is substantively different to Open Source. The change in name can probably also take some credit for the growing involvement of business in the movement, with many Open Source projects now involving significant business involvement and support.

We have now travelled far enough along this story to see how programmers and non-programmers can hack without programming. This is the inverse of the Lessig and Creative Commons story where non-programmers take hacking as an inspiration outside of hacking, here we have non-programmers who hack. Moglen, Raymond and others such as publisher Tim O'Reilly are emblematic figures of these social and cultural factors that permeate the programming that is the core of hacking. We could point out similar figures for cracking, for example the editor of the cracking magazine 2600 Emmanuel Goldstein (a pseudonym for Eric Corley inspired by George Orwell's writings); 2600 (www.2600.com) has been produced since 1984 and includes significant cracking information. Goldstein and others have also developed initiatives like the HOPE (Hackers on Planet Earth) conferences. Just as with FOSS, there are non-programmers hacking in cracking.

We have now seen two types of non-hacking in non-programmers who take the hack outside hacking and non-programmers who contribute to the hack. We can move to explore a third and significant category in programmers who do not hack even when writing code. This is clearest in the great software factories that corporations create to manufacture the code that constitutes proprietary software programmes.

The programming proletariat

Despite the power of Free and Open Source Software and despite the continuing engagement of crackers with breaking open computers and networks, the majority of coding activity is done by workers, by those employed to programme or to manage information technology security. Microsoft reported in 2007 that it employed 76,000 people worldwide, with around half of them in marketing and sales, leaving a programming force numbering tens of thousands (Microsoft 2007). And while Microsoft may be the largest programming company, there are several others with large staff; Oracle Corporation has around 50,000 total employees, Apple has just under 20,000. Alongside these giants are the myriad small companies offering everything from local services such as repairing or setting up small-scale home networks to start-up companies creating new products and looking to be the next Apple, Oracle or Microsft (Bronson 1999; Campbell-Kelly 2003). If we compare Free Software and Open Source programmers to those in corporations, then we should also recognise that crackers have their employed counterparts in the many programmers now working on anti-virus, firewall and other computer security industry products. Companies such as McAfee, Sophos and more general companies such as Microsoft, who also produce computer security products, are the worker counterparts of those crackers who make such security a widespread necessity.

The key point in relation to hacking is not just to recognise that hackers swim in a sea populated by many, many other programmers. This is an analytic distinction because it is perfectly possible to hack or crack in your spare time while being employed to programme in your work time, moreover given the need to earn a living and the fact that most hackers have programming expertise it is highly likely many hackers will be employed to programme. Further, the Open Source movement in particular has seen many hackers brought into corporations to develop Open Source products or even whole corporations (such as Red Hat or Suse) devoted to producing and maintaining Open Source products. The point to be made here is that programming does not make someone a hacker, and the most important and largest group of non-hacker programmers are those whose ability to define and redefine determinisms in computer and network technologies is not their own, but is decided by the institution that employs them. They can rightly be called the programming proletariat because they have had the key form of control that hackers 'own' – their ability to define, modify, make and contest informational technological determinisms – taken away from them and invested in corporate structures. The programming proletariat programme, they do not hack.

Yet the trappings of hacking surround the programming proletariat and draw them into an ideological relationship with hacking in which the truth that they are not hackers but programming proletariat is masked by various signs of hacking. Examples of this can be found in Microsoft's employment culture. One of the obvious indicators is that the main Microsoft factory, located in Redmond, Washington State, USA, is called a campus and is set out like a university campus. The buildings are set apart very much in the style of university campuses with green walkways between them and it is referred to as the Redmond campus. Also, the buildings and walkways are set amid a significant amount of forested land, in addition to the sculptured lawns. There are sports playing fields and a range of sports played, a fitness track and many of the signs one would expect from a US non-urban university campus. All this effort to look like something other than a factory attempts to place workers into a particular mindset which evokes the academic context of freedom, a freedom that is integral to hackers but fundamentally denied to programming proles.

Microsoft offers other markers of the hacking life than just an architecture that invokes the freedom of academia. Microsoft is noted for providing fridges full of highly caffeinated drinks, which invoke the image of frantic, hour upon hour coding sessions. They add other symbols of the dedicated, obsessed coder, particularly in the run up to the launch of major projects where they produce the juvenile fun of an end of term party. Microsoft run an annual puzzle hunt, drawing inspiration from the Massachusetts Institute of Technology Mystery Hunt, at which teams of employees, ex-employees and some outsiders are asked to solve complicated puzzles leading to a hidden treasure.

These, and other indicators, give all the signs of a freedom, particularly in their invocation of university life, that is fundamentally absent from the programmers at Microsoft, who programme to the needs of Microsoft and not to their own needs or the perceived needs of society or software. Microsoft programmers are coders who do not hack. This pattern is not universal but is repeated across the US-based software production world. Apple likes to trumpet its different organisational structure and all companies like to both cosset and then exploit their programmers as creative workers.

These characteristics make the programming proletariat very close to Lloyd's conception of the neo-bohemian who has to reconcile articulated opposition to various ideas with the employment of their labour to further these ideas. 'Rather than looking at artists as a resistant subculture, I became compelled to think of artists as useful labour, and to ask how their efforts are harnessed on behalf of interests that they often sincerely profess to despise' (Lloyd 2006: 239). Though coders in software factories will not always see themselves as being in opposition to their employer, they share the fate of neo-bohemians in appearing to the world to have an identity which is contradicted by their relationship to employment (Lloyd 2006: 205–32).

The masking of a lack of freedom in return for a wage is a tactic variably applied to many jobs under capitalism; Lloyd's neo-bohemia traces a relevant new variant of this. What is interesting in the current context is that it is to the signs of hacking that the great programming factories turn. This however is not necessarily true of other programmers who do not hack. There has been a significant internationalisation of programming work and here variable conditions apply. For example, one of the earliest extensions of programming by Western-based companies was Texas Instruments who in 1986 developed a twinned programming factory in Bangalore, India. The India-based coders passed on their work at the end of the day to an already established factory in Dallas, USA, allowing code to be developed continuously over 24 hours. Texas Instruments stated they came to India because they found there qualified software engineers who they could employ for about 10 per cent of the salaries of US-based engineers (Singhal and Rogers 2001: 170–1). Alongside these economic imperatives we can note how these programmers work on projects defined by the corporation and then send on whatever they have achieved to others, across the globe, so that 12 hours later revised code will appear again for them to work on. While Free Software and Open Source programmes are also developed collaboratively, the imposition of such a bureaucratic relationship underlines the corporate imperatives driving programmers who do not hack.

Such a shift from highly paid Western-based programmers working in coding factories, to distributed coding factories seeking out lower-paid expertise across the globe now seems characteristic of the software industry, and of course, of many other industries as well (Campbell-Kelly 2003). A small example is that Microsoft is now close to employing half its workforce overseas (46,000 US based and 30,000 overseas), though it retains a strong emphasis on its Redmond coding factory. The globalisation of the programming proletariat underlines that it is the corporations that choose, not the programmers. Whereas hackers engage with technological determinations of their choice and in their own ways, programmers are told by their corporations which technologies to engage with, under the ultimate aim of generating profit for the corporation. There should be nothing surprising about this, as it is the basic bargain nearly all employees in all industries strike, but it also distinguishes the vast majority of programmers from hackers.

Unlike many aspects of hacking, the programming proletariat have been immortalised in prose, in Douglas Coupland's novel *Microserfs*. This novel captures the sense in which programmers have been drawn closely into corporate desires while cloaking themselves in an ideology of hacking. The book heavily underlines the 'geek' and 'nerd' cultures of those working at Microsoft, who in the novel eventually move into their own independent start-up company, while also emphasising the emptiness of their programming ethics. Coupland counterposes skill, ethics and products in many passages.

> Susan's a real coding machine. But her abilities are totally wasted reworking old code for something like the Norwegian Macintosh version of Word 5.8. Susan's work ethic best sums

up the ethic of most of the people I've met who work at Microsoft. If I recall her philosophy from the conversations she had with her younger sister two weekends ago, it goes something like this:

'It's never been "We're doing this for the good of society." It's always been us taking an intellectual pride in putting out a good product – and making money. If putting a computer on every desktop and in every home didn't make money, we wouldn't do it.'

That sums up most of the Microsoft people I know.

(Coupland 1996: 9)

Such an ethos could hardly be enunciated by a hacker, not because it is impossible for hackers to be interested in making money out of hacking, but because Susan's skills are submerged within the corporate imperative to make money even if that means she ends up being a brilliant coder working on an insignificant project. This also helps make clear why it is entirely possible for people to be employed as programmers and to exist as hackers. If someone like the fictional Susan makes money out of programming, what is to stop her using any spare time to hack? Indeed, hacking may be compelling as a way of demonstrating her skills in projects she feels are more worthwhile. Coupland also captures the way the 'campus' ideology sweetens the bargain for programmers. Coupland's narrator summarises the intrusion of corporate into private life as posing the bargain: '*Give us your entire life or we won't allow you to work on cool projects*' (Coupland 1996: 211, emphasis in original). And cool projects have to be wrapped in the markers of hacking to be cool, even if they turn out to be reworking stale code for corporate profits.

Cultures and sub-cultures: cypherpunks, virus writers, hardware hackers, nerds and geeks

The programming proletariat allow us to see all the various permutations of hacking and programming. Creative Commons shows us non-programmers who do not hack, yet somehow take hacking's ethos into new realms. Moglen and Raymond show us non-programmers who do hack and who in their non-programming activities make important contributions to hacking. The programming proletariat offer us programmers who do not hack. The latter also separate out something we might call hacking culture, the symbols of being a hacker rather than the act of hacking. This connects to a number of loose ends in my overview of hacking that can be appropriately drawn together here. There is both a sense of hacking cultures, of ways of appearing to be a hacker without actually hacking, and of sub-cultures within hacking. The two can be usefully explored together because sub-cultures help illustrate what we take to be a hacking culture. I will therefore look at three examples of sub-cultures of hacking first, before turning to cultures of nerd and geek.

Sub-culture is an overworked concept in the social sciences and there is not the space or the need to detail it here (Hebdige 1981). The sense of sub-culture at play in the following is not complicated or sophisticated, at least by the standards of theories of sub-cultures. What is at stake is the way that sub-cultures involve a mutual recognition of allegiance to a particular culture within a culture, a 'sub' as in a subsidiary component of a broader culture (Thornton 1995).

Cypherpunks are one of the most obvious of such sub-cultures, a hacking sub-culture so strong cypherpunks may well have not seen themselves as a sub-culture at all. Cypherpunks have passed their peak with struggles that deeply concerned them in the 1990s giving way to a wider implementation of their ideas (and like the programming proletariat their concerns were central to a striking novel in Neal Stephenson's *Cryptonomicon*). Cypherpunks addressed growing issues of privacy produced by the Internet. This they saw as a twin-sided problem: first, how to produce anonymous transaction systems so that, just as when someone pays in cash, a digital exchange can occur but allow someone to remain private; second, how to authorise in the digital realm that a communication is from someone and how to keep that communication secret. Cypherpunks believed the answer to these problems was code that created digital encryption.

Encryption is the long-standing practice of scrambling messages so that only those who hold the key to the system can unscramble them. The digital age produced an innovation in encryption in public key cryptology, which is the counter-intuitive idea of an encryption system that allows keys to be public. Whitfield Diffie and Martin Hellman proposed a system whereby a mathematical process produces a digital key broken into two parts, public and private. The two keys are related mathematically such that the private key cannot be derived from the public key but a message encoded with the public key can only be decoded by the private key and a message encoded with the private key can only be decoded by the related public key. So if Alice encodes a message with her private key and sends it to Bob, then Bob can decode it with Alice's publicly available key and Bob will know that this message can only have come from Alice (Levy 2000: 66–89).

As these ideas were spreading during the 1990s, the US government in particular was concerned about the spread of high standards of encryption and sought to restrict their distribution. The provision of programmes, particularly Phil Zimmerman's Pretty Good Privacy, seemed to panic US security and intelligence agencies, leading to Zimmerman's prosecution and to the restrictions on exporting encryption techniques. The cypherpunks saw it as their mission to produce privacy through encryption in a context where governments seemed intent on preventing the spread of encryption, suggesting to the cypherpunks that governments did not want their citizens to be able to conduct private conversations. An online discussion list as well as face-to-face meetings thrived during this time and there were both media attention and significant coding going on. Cypherpunk Eric Hughes wrote a 'Cypherpunk Manifesto' in which he proclaimed:

We the Cypherpunks are dedicated to building anonymous systems. We are defending our privacy with cryptography, with anonymous mail forwarding systems, with digital signatures, and with electronic money.

Cypherpunks write code. We know that someone has to write software to defend privacy, and since we can't get privacy unless we all do, we're going to write it. We publish our code so that our fellow Cypherpunks may practice and play with it. Our code is free for all to use, worldwide. We don't much care if you don't approve of the software we write. We know that software can't be destroyed and that a widely dispersed system can't be shut down. . . .

The Cypherpunks are actively engaged in making the networks safer for privacy.

(Hughes 1993)

The connections to Free Software and Open Source ideas is clear in the desire to spread code and it is no surprise that some prominent cypherpunks were also prominent in Free and Open Source software (for example, John Gilmore). There is also in the cypherpunks the underlying ethos of hacking in their desire to code into the world of the Internet the possibility of encryption, so that their vision of privacy is always present, whether any other user of the Internet wants it to be or not. Cypherpunks, diminished activity and public profile mirrors the relaxing of government opposition to encryption and the widespread take up of such techniques by corporations and other entities seeking to use the Internet for commerce as well as for secure exchanges of information.

A different sub-culture is that of the Bulgarian virus writers. There have been a number of virus writing sub-cultures, some of them dedicated to destructive computer viruses but some dedicated to more intellectual pursuits and more likely to call their interests 'virtual life'. The latter is an area of study based on creating computer environments in which programmes can replicate themselves, mimicking evolutionary systems. Viruses have been written by a wide range of programmers, for various reasons, but there appeared in the 1990s a series of viruses all in some way connected with Bulgaria, leading to the assumption that they had been written there. Though little social or cultural history has been done on this particular group, Bulgarian anti-virus writer Vesselin Bontchev wrote a report detailing his view of the local culture of virus writing (Bontchev 1991).

Bontchev paints a picture of a range of viruses emerging from a growing group of virus writers in the late 1980s and 1990s. He argues that a well-educated but under-employed group of young people combined with a state policy that condoned if not promoted piracy (in order to crack and use Western software for free), as well as a total absence of criminal penalties for computer crime, created the preconditions for a group of virus writers. The well-known Dark Avenger was soon joined by Lubo, TP and a range of others who eventually communicated though a bulletin board system, the virus eXchange. The bulletin board stored copies of all viruses and allowed discussion between writers, but access to it was only given when an applicant provided a new virus – a rule that reflects cracking's intermingling of peer recognition and peer education. A sub-culture grew up that valued the viral properties of computer programmes and seemed astonished at the growing worldwide scope for infecting computers (Bontchev 1991). Bontchev claims a similar sub-culture emerged in Russia. The limitations of this picture are that though the problem of a series of viruses suddenly coming from Bulgaria, at least as measured by who signed them and other programming markers, was real, only Bontchev's analysis allowed us to picture the culture that most likely produced them.

Another sub-culture of hacking, which comes to grips with technologies in the most direct manner possible, is that of hardware hacking. This is the interference with products not in their software but by rewiring, resoldering and simply cutting up and reglueing the components of an existing piece of hardware. This type of hacking has long roots back beyond the emergence of computers in those who have enjoyed playing with technology, whether that be cars or horse saddles. This interest in reworking things was also engendered at the inception of hacking, with many early computer hackers being interested first in electronics and other gadgetry. Levy's famous story of the importance of the Tech Model Railway Club at the Massachusetts Institute of Technology in the 1960s shows this, as many early hackers met when working on the complicated electronics and hardware of the model railway (Levy 1984: 17–38).

Early developments in computing and networks often included hardware hacking in efforts to make things work as hackers wanted them to. For example, the precursor to the Internet was a network called Arpanet that worked by providing a computer, called an IMP (interface message processor) to each university participating in the network; each IMP talked from one end to the other IMPs and from their other end to a university's network. When the first IMP was delivered to the company implementing Arparnet (Bolt, Beranek and Newman, BBN) it did not work. The solution was some serious hardware hacking by Ben Barker.

> The circuitry of the computer relied on pin blocks, or wire-wrapped boards, that served as the central connection points to which wires, hundreds upon hundreds of wires, were routed. . . . After figuring out where the wires should actually go, Barker had to unwrap each tightly wound misconnected wire from its pin. The pins in each block were about an inch long and were closely spaced (1/20th of an inch apart) in a square matrix; each block looked like a miniature bed of nails with wires streaming Medusa-like into and out of it. Once he determined where the correct wires should be reconnected, Barker used the wire-wrap gun to wrap each wire carefully on its correct pin.
>
> (Hafner and Lyon 1996: 126–7)

The tradition of hardware hacking lives on in various ways, each of which consists of attacking and altering some piece of hardware. By the early twenty-first century the space for serious hardware hacking, like that of Barker on IMPs, was constrained by the greater involvement of corporations in making and selling hardware. Many hardware hacks have become whimsical, such as the people who alter their car tail lights to perform in patterns or the hacker who converts an Iphone into a Nintendo gaming console. Or if not meant as fun, they tend to serve a particular desire of a hardware hacker, for example in the use of Linux and a router to create a sprinkler system (see all of these at http://hackedgadgets.com). Hardware hackers take the spirit of hacking into material relations, finding new and novel uses enabled by the soldering iron rather than the command line.

From all these sub-cultures and the hackers of previous pages, an image of hackers as a certain type of person can be discerned: the nerd or geek. Ultrarational, poorly socialised and obsessive, the image of the nerd and geek has been transformed into a series of signs and behaviours which comprise a culture that some people buy into rather than live. By the early 1980s it was possible to stereotype nerds such that Hollywood could make a film called *Revenge of the Nerds*, equipping each fictional nerd with the most obvious of nerd symbols; such as glasses, bad dress sense and the most important of all nerd signs, the pocket protector. An example of nerd or geek behaviour, emphasising the rational over social convention is given by Levy:

> the logical mind-frame required for programming spilled over into more commonplace activities. . . . Marge Saunders would drive to the Safeway every Saturday morning in the Volkswagen and upon her return ask her husband, 'Would you like to help bring in the groceries?' Bob Saunders would reply, 'No'. Stunned, Marge would drag in the groceries herself. After the same thing occurred a few times, she exploded, hurling curses at him and demanding to know why he said no to her question.
> 'That's a stupid question to ask,' he said. 'Of course I won't like to help you bring in the groceries. If you ask me if I'll help you bring them in, that's another matter.'
> (Levy 1984: 36–7)

With the rise of the Internet and the ubiquity of computers, the geek or nerd look even extended to becoming a fashion, with the term 'geek chic' emerging to describe this. For example, the actor David Tennant has described the look created for his role as Dr Who as involving 'geek chic' (BBC 2005). Even when the geek or nerd is transformed into a time-travelling hero, the markers of intellectualism and odd dress sense remain (in this case, Converse sneakers underneath a rumpled suit and tie).

The production of a purely symbolic hacker means that hackers have become more easily integrated into popular culture. While I mentioned the film *Revenge of the Nerds* earlier, hackers have appeared now in many forms of popular culture, including novels, films, television and so on. Hackers have become a readily available villain, in such films as *Die Hard IV* and *Enemy of the State*, but also sometimes saintly heroes. The most obvious example of the latter is the *Matrix* trilogy in the first film of which Keanu Reeves' character Neo begins as a pale hacker who refuses to leave his room and lives by selling illicit digital merchandise, and at the end of the film undergoes a Christ-like resurrection from death after which he gains super-hero like powers for good.

In arriving at nerds and geeks we have moved beyond sub-cultures to touch on some elements of the overarching culture of hacking. We may seem to have arrived at some of the more trivial aspects of hacking, in the pocket protector or an actor's notion of geek chic, but these signs of hacking demonstrate the permeation of general cultures by hacking and indicate some of the non-rational aspects of hacking that also help to make it into a community, culture and movement.

Conclusion: cultures and sub-cultures

From the obsessively rational to the Creative Commons, this chapter has explored some of the further flung aspects of hacking. In this chapter, we have examined different permutations of programming, hacking and culture which move us at times beyond hacking. However, all the different phenomena we have explored over this and the previous chapter draw on the core mechanics created by the cracking community and the Free Software and Open Source movement and so they connect to and extend our view of hacking.

The popular stereotype of nerds and geeks as exemplified by Bob Saunders and whose look was codified in the film *Revenge of the Nerds* (white male, glasses, polyester trousers, short-sleeved shirt with a pocket protector, pale skin and poor haircut), reflects something that has only been briefly discussed so far in the male dominance of hacking. This is clearly a gender issue rather than a biological one, with there being many women who can programme and some few women who have played roles within hacking, but it remains the case that across all the different types of hacking that have been examined so far there is a strong male bias in membership. Hackers simply are in overwhelming numbers men.

What this means at an everyday level is relatively clear. For example, when a hacking conference is held there will be far more men than women attending. There are also, at first glance, examples of what seem to be deeper norms. For example, flaming (using deliberately abusive or hostile messages in online communication) is typical of online communities, including many parts of hacking and this can be hypothesised to be a consequence of competitive male habits. Yet we should be cautious of a simple equation of male bias and hacking. It is all too easy to impute stereotypical male characteristics to hackers (competitive, aggressive and poor emotional communication) and then to assume that this means there is misogyny in hacking. The presence of sexism, whether active or implicit in an unthinking male-dominated community, is highly likely but it is unclear whether hacking is any more or less affected than any other community that is male dominated; for example, among sporting clubs devoted to predominantly male sports. Without denying the male bias in hacking's membership or that it has consequences for behaviour, the point remains that it is not clear if this has anything to do with hacking itself or is simply some of the behaviour typical of male communities whatever the interest that constitutes that community. This is not to excuse or condone any such behaviour but to try and specify what might be particular to hacking. While male dominance must be kept in mind, the evidence is unclear how this relates to hacking in all but the most obvious ways.

We can now see a central dynamic around which a wide range of activities, some closer and some more distant, flow. This produces a varied and shifting view of hacking, which encompasses a wide range of disparate phenomena. The danger of this, and of the loose notions of community or movement that I have employed to characterise hacking, is that it is sometimes hard to see what it is that ultimately connects all the phenomena; can the term hacking really stretch from Richard Stallman to Kevin Mitnick and then on to the possible cyberterrorist and the actor playing a nerd? It is important now, having stretched hacking into many areas to demonstrate its variable and complex nature, to turn back and in the concluding chapter to outline what hacking means.

CHAPTER SIX

The Meaning of Hacking

Hacking

This investigation demonstrates that hacking relates to activities well beyond the media stereotype of the lone, and unkempt, teenage male obsessing over their computer in the search for illicit access to computers. At the same time, this investigation connects crackers and FOSS through a common explosion of social and technical relations of computer and network technologies. The evidence for both these claims lies in the preceding chapters.

One of the aims of this book has been to demonstrate the breadth of hacking, while at the same time defining what it is that constitutes hacking. The two aims pull in different directions, with the desire for breadth pulling examples further and further from what we might intuitively think is hacking, until we reach, for example, stereotyped film versions of nerds. Defining the core concerns of hacking leads to a narrower focus which keeps to the fore the activities of crackers and FOSS, while defining hacking's characteristic engagement with social and technological determinations enacted through computer and network technologies. I will look at each of these in turn, first summarising the complexity of hacking's material practices and then summing up hacking's central dynamic.

The world of hacking

Like all groups who do not have a formal membership but who have developed common social and cultural practices, norms and ethics, hacking is dispersed and unstable. Those who can be considered hackers move in and out of hacking practices, while different sub-groups blossom and fade. There is no way of identifying, once and for all, the final and true membership or organisational structure of hacking, no more than we could do for model train enthusiasts or mathematicians. There are, of course, formal hacking groups and organisations – for example the Free Software Foundation or the Chaos Computer Club – but these do not encapsulate or summarise hacking. As Maelstrom suggested, hacking is like a gossamer web.

What we can now see is that this web of ideas, ethics and actions has a particular structure and specific objects. I have argued that the central dynamics are constituted between the material practices of cracking and Free Software/Open Source. Around these central practices a range of other groups and actions have emerged that inter-weave with each other and the central dynamics, complicating and enriching hacking. This is not so much a matter of centre and periphery, as some of the non-cracking and non-FOSS actions can suddenly be at the centre of hacking (as cypherpunks were during encryption arguments). Rather, it is the dynamics of hacking that are set by cracking and FOSS, with other hackers and hacking groups drawing on this dynamic. I will explore more general conclusions about the social and cultural significance of hacking and digital media from this central dynamic below, here I am reviewing the material practices of hackers.

Cracking's material practices were explored under four different headings; zero-day exploit, zero-plus-one-day exploit, social engineering and script-kidding. Each of these describes a particular interaction between technologies and actions which allows a cracker illicit access to a targeted computer or the ability to in some way attack a computer. From ringing someone up and talking them out of their password and username to complex techniques for tricking computers into dropping their security, cracking takes as its object existing computers, networks and their configurations and alters them to the design of the cracker.

Free Software and Open Source programmes are built on practices of coding and programming in different organisational and dis-organisational forms. The lone coding prophet who returns from their time in the wilderness with new programmes is one type, though even such wizards are usually integrated within larger groups of hackers each dealing with some part of what are often complex and extensive programmes. A second type of dis-organisation is the collective programming efforts exemplified by Torvalds' leadership of Linux development. FOSS is fundamental to computers and networks, often operating at levels unseen by users (for example, BIND is the *de facto* standard domain name server which allows sites on the Internet to be located). FOSS pursues an explicit social agenda of keeping computers and networks that have become fundamental to society free and open.

Around these two key sets of material practices, we have seen a range of related practices that are relevant to an understanding of hacking. The interaction between cracking and FOSS, as well as other relevant activities, produces what I called the community of hacking. The practices that draw on cracking and FOSS need to be seen to understand the full complexity of hacking's community and these were grouped under the two themes of hacking the social and hacking the non-hack.

Hacking the social refers to a diverse range of practices all of which attempt to use hacking's characteristic attitude to social and technological interactions to change society. Hacktivists try to produce socio-technical interactions that promote grassroots or non-institutional political change, either through classic civil disobedience tactics adapted to the Internet or by embedding civil rights within Internet infrastructures. Cyberwarriors engage in state-sponsored attacks on other nation-states, utilising all the techniques offered by cracking. Cyberterrorists similarly utilise cracking techniques to try and change societies through fear. Cybercriminals seek, as is usual among criminals, to line their own pockets but in this case utilising electronic means.

Hacking the non-hack allows us to disentangle programming from hacking and from activities that are closely related to hacking but are not really hacks. The generation of new forms of property by Creative Commons seeks to take the inversions of property law created by the Free Software Foundation and apply them more generally. Non-programmers can be found within the core of hacking in publicity, legal work, organising and more. The programming proletariat work away in what often look like universities but which function as factories, compensated for not hacking by being paid and by being offered symbols of hacking. In addition, there are a range of often transient sub-cultures that I looked at in the cypherpunks and more. Out of this discussion of sub-cultures I argued that there is a set of symbols that represent the nerd and geek and that are able to be used outside of hacking to produce stereotypes of hackers. Hacking the non-hack shows us the effects of hacking spreading out beyond its concerns for computer and network technologies, while also allowing distinctions between programming and hacking to be clarified.

These widely varying material practices do not mean that hackers escape the constraints of twenty-first-century societies, any more than such societies can escape the effects of computer and networked information flows. We have seen in the programming proletariat how hacking can be used by corporations that have deep structural oppositions to hacking. Such corporations have begun to look at curbing free software, particularly attacking through patent laws. A patent exists when a government grants exclusive rights to use or sell an invention for a specified period and such inventions can be techniques used in software programmes (Goldstein 2003: 6). The most important example is Microsoft Corporation which has claimed that Linux violates 235 patents owned by Microsoft and has begun demanding payment for the use of these patents. Microsoft clearly has FOSS in its sights with these claims, looking to utilise the massive financial resources it has to begin containing what might be perceived as the threat Linux is posing to the long-term dominance of Microsoft's operating system. In an extension of this, Microsoft has been trying to make deals with corporations who use Linux in which Microsoft agrees not to sue the company for patent violations in return for royalties. Almost immediately after creating one of these deals, with Novell, Microsoft claimed it was proof that Novell admitted Linux infringed Microsoft's patents, something that Novell immediately denied. Novell's rebuttal of Microsoft's claim produces an odd situation because if Novell do not admit that they infringe any patents then paying Microsoft not to sue them over rights Novell claims Microsoft do not have, tends to lead many FOSS supporters to argue that Microsoft's tactic is effectively blackmail. Companies enter into such agreements and pay Microsoft royalties to prevent being involved in expensive litigation with an opponent who has almost limitless financial resources (Thurston 2007).

This example shows that hacking is not free of the conditions of twenty-first-century socio-economic structures. For example, we can see in this example how the 'Letter to Hobbyists' written by Bill Gates back in 1976 (discussed in chapter 1), in which Gates argued software needed to be subject to exclusive notions of property, returns to struggle with FOSS's attempt to recreate property as distribution. We could also find other examples such as police crackdowns on crackers, with many nation-states forming dedicated high-technology crime squads. Or there are the ongoing struggles by hacktivists to create secure communications, as some nation-states seek to restrict access to information in new ways.

We should not see the material practices of hackers as floating free, somehow affecting the world outside hacking but not being subject to it. Instead, though the focus of these arguments has been to define hacking, it is important to remember that the nature of hacking engages with all the myriad social forces flowing through twenty-first-century societies. If the arguments of this book have not focused on defining those social forces then that is simply because the present work is about defining hacking, not engaging in the far more complex task of defining society, but the socially embedded nature of hacking should not be forgotten.

The varied set of material practices undertaken by hackers emphasises the variety and complexity of hacking, even if at each point the practices focus on the capabilities of computer and network technologies. This is true even for non-programming hacking practices such as the GPL. Hackers, in one way or another and sometimes indirectly, hack computers and networks. Yet, as hacking itself demonstrates, stabilising social groups by reference to a material object or objects is a weak tactic. Hackers are devoted to changing the nature of computers and networks and this destabilisation of the object makes any seeming material solidity phantasmic. Rather, the object is the site of processes of social and technical negotiation, just as we saw in the way the question 'does it run?' provides a site of negotiated closure for FOSS projects. To complete this picture of hacking we need to turn away from a focus on specific material practices and ally those practices to the social and cultural changes they make. We need to consider the meaning of hacking digital media in the twenty-first century.

Hacking the world

Material practices of such variety as those already outlined suggest not just that hacking is complex but that it is incoherent; by doing legal work someone does not need to programme to hack, with social engineering one does not need to touch a computer to crack. Perhaps my account could now be accused of a version of the conceptual incoherence I accuse Wark and Himanen of creating when they argue that to hack is to make differences or be creative (see chapter 1). I have claimed so many different material practices as relevant to hacking, does this mean that the term has lost meaning? To refute this claim I need to shift back to the arguments I have been making over the meaning of technology, society and determinations that have been threaded through the previous chapters.

The beginning point of this argument was that hacking makes redundant the long-standing problem of technological determinism. I have claimed that hacking both demands and refutes technological determinism. This is a position which contradicts both those who argue in favour of technological determinism and those who in refuting technological determinism have ensured we see technologies as socially shaped. These latter arguments draw on a complex history of empirical and theoretical work in the social studies of science and technology, which there is no space to adequately recount here (Mackenzie and Wajcman 1999). Instead, I wish to consider quickly what technological determinism means and then outline how it is that hacking overcomes this problem, setting new terms for discussing relations between society and technology.

As Winner points out in his classic discussion of technological determinism, almost nobody holds the extreme view of technological determinism that requires two hypotheses: '(1) that the technical base of society is the fundamental condition affecting all patterns of social existence and (2) that changes in technology are the single most important source of change in society.' (Winner 1977: 76). Yet many people hold slightly less extreme versions in which technology conditions the range of choices societies make and in which changed technologies figure as key explanations for changed societies. Such versions still posit a form of causation between technologies and the nature of societies and therefore leave the issue of technological determinism intact. As already noted, extensive work in the social studies of technology has established that technologies are themselves socially caused. This in turn finally established technological determinism as an incorrect argument because technologies are not outside of society and so cannot simply cause social change (Mackenzie and Wajcman 1999).

Into this conceptual situation I have drawn the nature of hacking, which I have argued both assumes and works with reciprocal determinations between technology and society. Hackers presume the technologies involved in computers and networks will determine certain actions and they presume also it is possible for them to alter and recreate such determinations. They work here in ways that impossibly intertwine politics and technology, while also being clear about the ways the two separate and affect each other. For example, the cracker MacKinnon was working to a political motive, acting, he thought, to uncover hidden information so that free energy could be unleashed into the world. Any FOSS hacker is producing a programme which embodies a politics of open access to source code, while simultaneously producing for the world something functional like a word processor or web-server software.

Hacking poses the problem that technology and society cannot be separated but nor can they be kept together. Hacking assumes both that technology determines society and society determines technology. The conceptual difficulty hacking poses is the simultaneous separation and merging of technology and society, in a context where each is held to be able to determine the other. It is this complexity that hacking has at its heart and which defines hacking. The answer to how such a set of contradictions does not collapse is that hackers are able to shift between each possible state these elements can produce, holding a state stable or taking it for granted, even while their practices presume that particular state can be made unstable.

There are two ways of developing the implications of this fundamental dynamic of hacking that are important. The first is to go into some further conceptual work. My definitions so far have been relying perhaps a little too much on fairly simple understandings of what is meant by 'technology', 'society' and most importantly 'determination'. The second direction is to reflect on what hacking means for humanity's relationship with technology. What general consequences for all of us might be made clearer by this exploration of hacking? Are there conclusions relevant to the nature of twenty-first-century societies that hacking helps us to see? The first of these I will consider here, while the second will be discussed below.

Much of the preceding argument has relied on some notion of causation between technology and society and it is important to begin by examining this relationship. There also already exists relevant conceptual work that takes a very similar starting point in the difficulties posed by entirely dismissing the idea of technological determinism, as many social studies of technology would lead us to do. This is so in Hutchby's work on the application of the concept of 'affordances' from psychology to technology.

Hutchby begins from a similar point in relation to technological determinism as I do. He pushes social studies of technology arguments to the point where he takes issue with 'certain aspects of the recent radical sociology of technology, centred as it is around an uneasy social constructivist consensus. The main thrust of this consensus has cast into doubt the very validity of asking questions about the nature of technologies and communications, and the impacts of technologies on social life' (Hutchby 2001: 3). Hutchby's argument is that social studies of technology have proven technology is socially shaped, but this means that technology has disappeared into society and can no longer be analysed. He notes particularly that any attempt to analyse technology can be met with the accusation of technological determinism but that this leaves technologies unmarked by any analysis specific to them.

Hutchby's point is not that many social studies of technology are entirely wrong, though he takes issue with some theorists he considers have taken extreme positions (Hutchby 2001: 23–5), but that instead of enabling technology to be subject to social analysis, social studies of technology have eliminated such analysis thereby also eliminating analysis of the effects technologies have within society. This is very similar to the conceptual position I have argued that analysing hacking produces, in which the accusation of technological

determinism seems to contradict what I have argued constitutes the nature of hacking. From an entirely different line of
inquiry, I have arrived at a similar conceptual need as Hutchby
identifies, in the need for means to analyse the particular
effects of technologies and their determinations without falling
back into a simplistic form of technological determinism.
Hutchby's answer is the concept of affordances:

> But the inevitable question that then arises is: does the aero-
> plane lend itself to the same set of possible interpretations as
> the bridge, and if not, why not? . . . It seems clear that the
> answer to this question is no. The reason is that different tech-
> nologies posses different *affordances*, and these affordances
> constrain the way that they can be read. . . . The concept of
> affordances is associated with the work of Gibson in the psy-
> chology of perception. For Gibson, humans, along with ani-
> mals, insects, birds and fishes, orient to objects in their world
> (rocks, trees, rivers, etc.) in terms of what he calls their
> affordances: the possibilities that they offer for action. . . .
> Affordances may differ from species to species and from con-
> text to context. However, they cannot be seen as freely variable.
> While a tree offers an enormous range of affordances for a
> vast variety of species, there are things a river can afford which
> the tree cannot, and vice versa.
>
> (Hutchby 2001: 26)

Technologies are neither socially neutral nor are they solely
and entirely the result of social forces; technologies both con-
strain and produce possibilities for action in specific contexts.
Affordances allow analysis of technologies to take account of
the particular nature of individual technologies and their social
contexts, while at the same time not reducing the actors who
interact with technology to being mere by-products of that
technology. Technologies have capabilities.

> Does this reference to capabilities not mean that there are,
> after all, the kinds of determinate properties to technologies
> which social constructivists argue against? In a way it does. To
> focus on affordances in the way I suggest *is* to accept that
> there are features of artefacts that are not constructed

through accounts. In my view, it is these features that provide
the very conditions of possibility for competing accounts to
be sensibly made. However, this is not to fall back into a form
of technological determinism, because it is not to claim that
human actors are necessarily caused to react in given ways to
technological forms.

(Hutchby 2001: 29)

There is, however, a tension within Hutchby's account between
accepting some of the conclusions of social studies of technology that technologies are socially shaped while at the same time
retaining some notion of determination that flows from a technology. This is a finely balanced account that at the moment
appears to rely on pulling together some contradictory positions – that technological determinism is incorrect while at the
same time asserting that technologies do determine.

In my view, this balance is largely maintained because affordances operate on actions, that is at the everyday level. Hutchby
does not emphasise this point, though it is implicit in his arguments and certainly underpins his style of empirical analysis
which emphasises micro-moments of interaction. 'The affordances of an artefact are not things which impose themselves
upon humans' actions with, around or via that artefact. But they
do set limits on what it is *possible* to do with, around or via the
artefact' (Hutchby 2001: 33). These moments when it is possible
to do something with a technology, but not possible to do anything with a technology, are the moments when affordances
come into play, but they are moments. This places affordances in
the midst of everyday living and interacting with technology; this
is the moment when a cracker enters commands, the moment
when a FOSS programmer forwards a patch to improve a programme, this is the moment a website collapses under a flood
attack; these are moments that exist in the everyday.

Locating affordances at the everyday allows the balance to be
maintained within Hutchby's account because if we are all
determined and able to determine technologies in everyday
moments then it is possible to simultaneously reflect on a

higher level of abstraction in which we know that technologies are fundamentally social. The contradiction or tension that I have suggested is implicit in Hutchby's account, is between the ways we all interact with technology at an everyday level – those moments when a technology like this computer allows me to type but does not, as yet, make me a cup of coffee – and social science abstractions which explore the ways all technologies are constituted out of embedded social relations.

Recognising these different levels and so being able to integrate accounts of both technological determination and of the social nature of technology together, is a shift for social sciences which can result from examining hacking. It is also an important shift because social studies of technology have become increasingly unable to understand why technological determinism is so recurrent and compelling a view of the world. But the present account shows that technological determinism is an everyday occurrence for anyone who uses a technology and thus forms an experiential basis for the idea of technological determinism. We can in this way understand why so many find technological determinism at a social level – steam power caused industrial society, computers cause information societies – a compelling view because, when nearly everyone is subject to recurrent everyday experiences of being determined by technologies, technological determinism seems to make sense even though at a societal level is it mistaken.

A final point concerning the meaning of hacking's constitution of society, technology and determination or affordances in relation to each other emerges at this point. Affordances conceptualise not the experience of a technology forcing someone to do one and only one thing, but the experience of being presented with only some possibilities and prevented from taking up some other possibilities. As Hutchby emphasises, actors are creative with technologies meaning that technologies afford users a range of possibilities, including unexpected possibilities, but this does not mean any individual technology affords all possibilities. Affordance is about production and restriction, it is a form of power as Foucault conceived power in relation to the emergence of Western penality. 'This power is not exercised simply as an obligation or a prohibition on those who "do not have it"; it invests them, is transmitted by them and through them; it exerts pressure upon them, just as they themselves, in their struggle against it, resist the grip it has on them'(Foucault 1977: 27).

Affordances are a form of power. Determination remains a key component of affordances, for an account of affordances which neutralises the politics of which possibilities are possible by eliminating ideas about determination will also eliminate the ability to see the relations of power produced by technologies. Determination involves a sense of causation that can seem absent within a washed-out interpretation of affordances, determination reinforces the sense that technologies determine only certain social actions as being possible and in this way 'determination' more clearly than the term 'affordance' opens up the political and power dimensions of technology.

When FOSS programmers create a complex set of software and release it free with the GNU Public Licence attached they intervene in the politics and power of their society by changing the nature of property and creativity. The GPL determines that only certain actions can be taken around whichever software it is attached to; it constrains someone from altering the programme and then closing that programme down, and it allows open access to the source code allowing further actions taken by programmers to change the code. These inter-weaving affordances, in this case both legal and technological, constitute part of power and politics in relation to FOSS. We could multiply the examples of inter-relations of affordances both for other parts of hacking and we could extend the discussion to other socio-technologies. In this way hacking opens up new strategies for social scientific analyses of power in society and technology. However, these avenues are beyond present arguments; it is enough to note that it is the idea of determination embedded within the concept of everyday affordances that opens up analysis of power and politics.

At the heart of hacking is this dynamic and mutual determination between society and technology. Such fluidity is characteristic of the digital nature of computers and networks because it is so much easier to alter the technologies and social possibilities of software than of many other technologies. The virtual nature of software, its constant malleability because it is native to digital media, allows this shifting between technological and societal determinations. It is this ability to hold seemingly contradictory forms of causation within the one dynamic that marks hacking as hacking.

The implications for social science are that the problem of technological determination of society or of social determination of technologies is dissolved within digital media. It is dissolved not in the sense that the terms the problematic uses – society, technology, determination – are meaningless, but in the sense that contradictory positions can be simultaneously maintained and maintaining such contradictions proves highly dynamic and effective. The concept of affordances gives conceptual substance to this position. Hacking is part of social change, including change in social sciences.

Humanity and technology

There is no humanity without technology. From the simplest of sticks to poke the earth or branches pulled together into a shelter to the skyscrapers and de-materialising communications of the Internet, there is no human society without technologies characteristic to it.

Humanity is not determined by technologies but it is, in part, both created and restrained by technologies. The interplay of such creativity and restraint has often been interpreted as a debate between technological determinists – steam power equals the birth of industrial society – and anti-technological determinists – industrial society created steam power. Though both sides can put more sophisticated versions of their argument than a simple causal arrow from either society or technology to, respectively, technology or society, the fundamental intellectual structure that haunts and frames both academic and popular debate in relation to technology is this model of causation.

Hackers show us this frame is misleading. The hack relies on being created and restrained by certain technologies that are taken for granted while simultaneously creating new technological restraints according to the social and political imperatives of hackers. Being determined in the sense of having only certain options that a technology allows and being able to determine through technology, by changing a technology's functions, is taken for granted among hackers. Such a state is simply the state of being with technology, especially digital media.

Hacking is a crucial component of twenty-first-century societies for a number of reasons. Hackers are intimately involved in making some of the fundamental technologies of our time. Hackers are inventing and testing new political, military and criminal forms. Hacking is being drawn out further and further into cultural realms, allowing the signifiers of hacking to be attached to things that are not hacks. Yet, across all these activities which mark hacking's relationship to political, economic and cultural structures, there is an underlying and fundamental point made by the nature of hacking in its redrawing of humanity's relationship to technology, from whether there are determinations or not to constantly developing sets of determinative affordances in computer and network socio-technologies.

Further reading (all sources mentioned are in the list of references)

For further reading about cracking there are two avenues. The first is academic analyses and the second is popular journalistic accounts. Among academic accounts there is no better grounded analysis than Paul Taylor, *Hackers: crime in the digital sublime*, even given that this was published in 1999. Thomas's *Hacker culture* has a mainly cracking focus and has some interesting discussion of hacking and popular culture. Journalistic accounts tend towards the fantastic story, sometimes mythologising, but nevertheless producing some impressively researched stories. Though new stories are likely to appear at the same time as this book is being published there are already a few classics in this genre of which Hafner and Markoff's *Cyberpunk*, Littman's duo *The Fugitive Game* and *The Watchman* and Freedman's and Mann's *At Large* stand out for me. Mitnick's and Simon's *The Art of Intrusion* is a hybrid with practical advice, many stories and some conceptualisation of cracking.

FOSS is less well served, though it can be expected to receive growing attention. The stand out academic book is Weber's *The Success of Open Source*, which no-one interested in FOSS should ignore. In a more populist and historical vein Moody's *Rebel Code* is excellent; even though it is focused on Linux it fills in much of the story of Free Software and Open Source. Gillespie's *Wired Shut* takes up many issues posed by FOSS and property relations and makes strong connections to cultural studies.

For the other elements of hacking there are a range of sources. My own and Paul Taylor's *Hacktivism: rebels with a cause*, presents a detailed social scientific overview of hacktivism. The two collections Webster, *Culture and Politics in the Information Age* and van de Donk et al., *Cyberprotest* cover much of the ground of the Internet and activist politics. I know of no single text which gives a good account of cyberwar, either academic or populist and cannot offer a strong recommendation here; though Everard's *Virtual States* is good on the changes to the state including issues of war, and De Landa's *War in the Age of Intelligent Machines* is often used as a conceptual starting point, despite its age. The best source on cyberterror is Weimann's *Terror on the Internet*, and there really is no competitor given its wide coverage and reasonable approach in an area fraught with hype and exaggeration. Cybercrime has been more widely studied and many of the texts on crackers are also relevant here. Wall's work on cybercrime is very strong and his book *Cybercrime* is easily the stand-out work on this topic, though Yar's *Cybercrime and Society* is also good.

The debate around Creative Commons is best approached through Lessig's own work, which is both accessible and presents strong arguments. Probably the best way in to his arguments is *The Future of Ideas* though *Free Culture* covers similar ground and is more recent. Benkler's *The Wealth of Nations* covers similar arguments but with a wider view of society and perhaps with a bit more objectivity. The programming proletariat are poorly served with analyses of their status. Bronson's *The Nudist on the Late Shift* is an amusing populist account but Coupland's novel *Microserfs* probably remains the best introduction to the world of the coding factory. Campbell-Kelly's *From Airline Reservations to Sonic the Hedgehog* is the classic academic account of the nature of the software industry, but it offers little insight into the cultural factors so important to hacking and the programming proletariat. Cypherpunks have been covered though not in much detail by academics; their story is well told in journalistic fashion by Levy's *Crypto* and in a fictional form by Stephenson's novel *Cryptonomicon* (and a not very relevant tip is that if you like *Cryptonomicon* then do not under any circumstances miss out on Stephenson's trilogy *The Baroque Cycle*).

No doubt I have missed some useful and important books; there will certainly be a lot more published in the future in these areas and this list is biased toward my own tastes and reading. Still, it offers many avenues forward on the many dimensions of hacking.

References

Abbate, J. (2000) *Inventing the Internet*, Cambridge, Mass.: MIT Press

AFP (2005) 'Hacker attacks in US linked to Chinese military: researchers', available at www.breitbart.com/article.php?id= 051212224756.jwmkvntb&show_article=1, accessed June 2007

Anderson, B. (1983) *Imagined Communities: reflections on the origins and spread of nationalism*, London: Verso

Anon (2007) 'Nobody knows you're a dog: Blog', available at http://blogs.law.harvard.edu/anonymous/2007/02/26/the-rumors-of-our-demise/, accessed June 2007

Barnes, B. (2000) *Understanding Agency: social theory and responsible action*, London: Sage

BBC (2005) 'Filming Starts : Christmas comes early for Dr Who', available at www.bbc.co.uk/doctorwho/news/cult/news/drwho/2005/07/25/20751.shtml, accessed August 2007

Benkler, Y. (2006) *The Wealth of Networks: how social production transforms markets and freedom*, London: Yale University Press

Bernstein, J. (2003) 'Bogus popularity claims for Sendmail', available at http://cr.yp.to/surveys/sendmail.html, accessed February 2007

Bontchev, V. (1991) 'The Bulgarian and Soviet virus factories', available at www.people.frisk-software.com/~bontchev/papers/factory.html, accessed August 2007

Bronson, P. (1999) *The Nudist on the Late Shift: and other tales of Silicon Valley*, New York: Secker and Warburg

Camera Shy (2007) 'Camera shy on sourceforge', available at http://sourceforge.net/projects/camerashy/, accessed June 2007

Campbell-Kelly, M. (2003) *From Airline Reservations to Sonic the Hedgehog: a history of the software industry*, Cambridge, Mass.: MIT Press

Castells, M. (2000) *The Rise of the Network Society: the information age, Volume One, 2nd edition*, London: Blackwell

CAE (Critical Arts Ensemble) (1994) *The Electronic Disturbance*, New York: Autonomedia

CAE (Critical Arts Ensemble) (1996) *Electronic Civil Disobedience and Other Unpopular Ideas*, New York: Autonomedia

Coupland, D. (1996) *Microserfs*, London: HarperCollins

daemon9/route/infinity (1996) 'IP-spoofing demystified: trust-relationship exploitation', *Phrack*, 48, available at www.citi.umich.edu/u/provos/security/ph48.txt, accessed June 2006

Denning, D. (2001) 'Is cyber terror next?', available at www.ssrc.org/sept11/essays/denning.htm, accessed July 2007

De Landa, M. (1992) *War in the Age of Intelligent Machines*, New York: Zone Books

Der Derian, J. (2001) *Virtuous War: mapping the military-industrial-media-entertainment network*, Boulder, CO: Westview

Dibona, C., Ockman, S. and Stone, M. (eds.) (1999) *Open Sources: voices from the revolution*, Sebastopol, CA: O'Reilly

Dittrich, D. (1999) 'The "stacheldraht" distributed denial of service tool', *Global Incident Analysis Centre*, available at www.sans.org/y2k/stacheldraht.htm, accessed 09/06/2006

Drogin, B. (1999) 'Russians seem to be hacking into Pentagon', SanFrancisco Chronicle, available at www.sfgate.com/cgi-bin/article.cgi?file=/chronicle/archive/1999/10/07/MN58558.DTL, accessed June 2007

Eazel, W. (2006) ' "Fat Spaniard" hacker faces forty years in jail', *SC Magazine*, 11 April, available at www.scmagazine.com/us/news/article/553114/fat+spaniard+hacker+faces+40+years+jail/, accessed July 2007

Everard, J. (2000) *Virtual States: the Internet and the boundaries of the nation-state*, London: Routledge

Foucault, M. (1977) *Discipline and Punish: the birth of the prison*, Harmondsworth: Penguin

Freedman, D. and Mann, C. (1997) *At Large: the strange case of the world's biggest Internet invasion*, New York: Simon and Schuster

Friedel, S. (2005) 'SQL injection attacks by example', *Steve Freidel's Unixwix.net Tech Tips*, available at www.unixwiz.net/techtips/sql-injection.ht, accessed June 2006

Gates, B. (1976) 'An open letter to hobbyists', available at http://en.wikipedia.org/wiki/Open_Letter_to_Hobbyists, accessed February 2007

Gillespie, T. (2007) *Wired Shut: copyright and the shape of digital culture*, Cambridge Mass.: MIT Press

Goldstein, P. (2003) *Copyright's Highway: from Gutenberg to the celestial jukebox*, Stanford: Stanford University Press

Gow, D. and Norton-Taylor, R. (1996) 'Surfing superhighwaymen', *The Guardian*, 7/12/1996, p. 28

GPL v.3 (2007) GNU Public License Version 3, available at www.gnu.org/licenses/, accessed July 2007

Hacktivismo (2006) 'Hacktivismo releases Torpark', available at www.hacktivismo.com, accessed May 2007

Hafner, K. and Lyon, M. (1996) *Where Wizards Stay Up Late: the origins of the Internet*, New York: Simon and Schuster

Hafner, K. and Markoff, J. (1991) *Cyberpunk: outlaws and hackers on the computer frontier*, London: Corgi

Hebdige, D. (1981) *Subculture: the meaning of style*, London: Routledge

Himanen, P. (2001) *The Hacker Ethic: a radical approach to the philosophy of business*, New York: Random House

Hughes, E. (1993) 'A cypherpunk's manifesto', available at www.activism.net/cypherpunk/manifesto.html, accessed August 2007

Hutchby, I. (2001) *Conversation and Technology: from the telephone to the Internet*, Cambridge: Polity

Jordan, T. and Taylor, P. (1998) 'A sociology of hackers', *Sociological Review*, 46 (4): 757–88

Jordan, T. (2002) *Activism!: direct action, hacktivism and the future of society*, London: Reaktion

Jordan, T. and Taylor, P. (2004) *Hacktivism and Cyberwars: rebels with a cause?*, London: Routledge

Kane, P. (1989) *V.I.R.U.S protection*, New York: Random House

Kelly, S. (2006) 'Hacker fears UFO cover-up: interview with Gary McKinnon', BBC Online, available at http://news.bbc.co.uk/1/hi/programmes/click_online/4977134.stm, accessed June 2007

Lessig, L. (2001) *The Future of Ideas: the fate of the commons in a connected world*, New York: Vintage Books

Lessig, L. (2004) *Free Culture: how big media uses technology and the law to lock down culture and control creativity*, New York: Penguin Press

Levy, S. (1984) *Hackers: heroes of the computer revolution*, London: Penguin

Levy, S. (2000) *Crypto: secrecy and privacy in the new code war*, London: Penguin

Leyden, J. (2003) 'Office workers give away password for a cheap pen', *The Register*, 18 April, available at www.theregister.co.uk/2003/04/18/office_workers_give_away_passwords/, accessed August 2007

Littman, J. (1996) *The Fugitive Game: online with Kevin Mitnick*, New York: Little, Brown and Co

Littman, J. (1997) *The Watchman: the twisted life and crimes of serial hacker Kevin Poulson*, New York: Little, Brown and Co

Lloyd, R. (2006) *Neo-Bohemia: art and commerce in the postindustrial city*, London: Routledge

Mackenzie, D. and Wajcman, J. (eds.) (1999) *The Social Shaping of Technology*, 2nd edition, Maidenhead: Open University Press

Meikle, G. (2002) *Future Active: media activism and the Internet*, London: Routledge

Melucci, A. (1996) *Challenging Codes: collective action in the information age*, Cambridge: Cambridge University Press

Microsoft (2007) 'Fast facts about Microsoft', updated 26 March 2007', available at www.microsoft.com/presspass/insidefacts_ms.mspx#E3CAE, accessed August 2007

Mitnick, K. D. and Simon, W. L. (2005) *The Art of Intrusion: the real stories behind the exploits of hackers, intruders and deceivers*, Indianapolis: Wiley Publishing

Modine, A. (2007) 'Hacker breaks into Pentagon mail system', *The Register*, 22 June, available at www.theregister.com/2007/06/22/department_of_defense_email_hacked/, accessed August 2007

Moody, G. (2001) *Rebel Code: Linux and the Open Source revolution*, London: Penguin

Moody, G. (2006) 'A lawyer who is also idealist: how refreshing', *The Guardian* 30 March 2006, available at www.guardian.co.uk/technology/2006/mar/30/guardianweeklytechnology/section.law, accessed July 2007

Netcraft (2007) 'January 2007 web server survey', available at http://news.netcraft.com/archives/2007/01/05/january_2007_web_server_survey.html, accessed February 2007

Nissenbaum, H. (2004) 'Hackers and the contested ontology of cyberspace', *New Media and Society*, 6(2): 195–217

Norton-Taylor, R. (2007) 'Titan Rain: how Chinese hackers targeted Whitehall', *The Guardian*, 5 September 2007, p. 1

O'Day, A. (ed.) (1995) *Terrorism's Laboratory: the case of Northern Ireland*, Aldershot: Dartmouth

Out-Law News (2007) 'Bank hit by "biggest ever" hack', *Out-Law News*, available at www.out-law.com/page-7679, accessed July 2007

Pilkington, E. and Johnson, B. (2007) 'China flexes muscles of its "informationised" army', *The Guardian*, 5 September 2007, p. 12

Quartermain, J. (1990) *The Matrix: computer networks and conferencing systems worldwide*, Bedford: Digital Press

Raymond, E. S. (2001) *The Cathedral and the Bazaar: musing on Linux and Open Source by an accidental revolutionary*, 2nd edition, Sebastopol, CA: O'Reilly

Raymond, E. S. (1999) 'Shut up and show them the code', *Linux Today*, 28 June 1999, available at www.linuxtoday.com/news_story. php3?ltsn=1999–06–28–023–10-NW-SM, accessed July 2007

Scatterchat (2007) 'Scatterchat', available at www.scatterchat.com/, accessed June 2007

Shimomura, T. (1995) *Takedown: the pursuit and capture of Kevin Mitnick*, with John Markoff, New York: Secker and Warburg

Singhal, A. and Rogers, E. M. (2001) *India's Communication Revolution: from bullock carts to cyber marts*, London: Sage

Smith, M. (1995), 'Holding fire: strategic theory and the missing military dimension in the academic study of Northern Ireland', in A. O'Day (ed.) (1995) *Terrorism's Laboratory: the case of Northern Ireland*, Aldershot: Dartmouth, pp. 225–40

Sooman, D. (2005) 'Oregon man pleads guilty in Ebay DDOS attack', *Techspot*, available at www.techspot.com/news/19945-oregon-man-pleads-guilty-in-ebay-ddos-attack.html, accessed June 2006

Stallman, R. (1999) 'The GNU operating system and the Free Software movement', in C. Dibona *et al.* (eds) (1999) *Open Sources: voices from the revolution*, Sebastopol, CA: O'Reilly, pp. 53–70

Sterling, B. (1992) *The Hacker Crackdown: law and disorder on the electronic frontier*, New York: Viking

Studdert, D. (2005) *Conceptualising Community: beyond the state and the individual*, London: Palgrave Macmillan

Tanase, M. (2003) 'IP Spoofing: an introduction', *Security Focus*, available at www.securityfocus.com/infocus/1674, accessed June 2006

Taylor, M. (2007) 'Divorce, wealth and hi-tech snooping: court hears of world of secret software', *The Guardian*, 26 April, p. 9

Taylor, P. (1999) *Hackers: crime in the digital sublime*, London: Routledge

Thomas, D. (2002) *Hacker Culture*, Minneapolis: University of Minnesota Press

Thomas, D. and Loader, B. (eds.) (2001) *Cybercrime: law enforcement, security and surveillance in the information age*, London: Routledge

Thomas, J. (2004) 'The moral ambiguity of social control in cyberspace: a retro-assessment of the "golden age" of hacking', *New Media and Society*, 7(5): 599–624

Thornton, S. (1995) *Club Cultures: music, media and subcultural capital*, Cambridge: Polity

Thomson, I. (2007) 'Russia hired 'Botnets' for Estonia cyber-war', available at www.infowar-monitor.net/modules.php?op=modload&name=News&file=article&sid=1398, accessed June 2007

Thurston, R. (2007) 'Ballmer repeats threat against Linux', CNET News.com, available at www.news.com/2100-7344-3-6160604.html, accessed November 2007

TJF (2006) The On-line Hacker Jargon File, 4.4.7, available at www.catb.org/jargon/index.html, accessed April 2006

Tomlinson, R. (2006) 'The first network email', available at http://openmap.bbn.com/~tomlinso/ray/firstemailframe.html, accessed April 2006

Torvalds, L. (2007) 'Re: dual-licensing Linux Kernel with GPL V2 and GPL V3' , post to Linux Kernel mailing list 10 June 2007, available at www.ussg.iu.edu/hypermail/linux/kernel/0706.1/0972.html, accessed July 2007

Torvalds, L. (2001) 'Prologue: what makes hackers tick? a.k.a. Linus's Law', in P. Himanen (2001), The Hacker Ethic: a radical approach to the philosophy of business, New York: Random House, pp. xiii–xvii

Torvalds, L. with Diamond, D. (2001) Just for Fun: the story of an accidental revolutionary, New York: Texere

Traynor, I. (2007) 'Russia accused of unleashing cyberwar to disable Estonia', The Guardian, 17 May, pp. 1–2

Turkle, S. (1984) The Second Self: computers and the human spirit, London: Granada

van de Donk, W., Loader, B., Nixon, P. and Rucht, D. (eds.) (2004) Cyberprotest: new media, citizens and social movements, London: Routledge

Verton, D. (2003) Black Ice: the invisible threat of cyber-terrorism, New York: McGraw-Hill

Viegas, F., Wattenberg, M. and Dave, K. (2004) 'Studying cooperation and conflict between authors with history flow visualizations', CHI 2004, 6 (1): 575–82

Wall, D. S. (2001) 'Cybercrimes and the Internet' in D. S. Wall (ed.) (2001) Crime and the Internet, London: Routledge, pp. 1–17

Wall, D. S. (ed.) (2001) Crime and the Internet, London: Routledge

Wall, D. S. (2007) Cybercrime: the transformation of crime in the information age, Cambridge: Polity

Wark, McKenzie (2004) A Hacker Manifesto, Cambridge, Mass.: Harvard University Press. (This text is written as numbered epigrams without numbered pages, references are therefore to the epigrams.)

Watts, J. (2007) 'Army sets sights on targets in space and cyberspace', The Guardian, p. 12–13

Weber, Steven (2004) The Success of Open Source, Harvard: Harvard University Press

Webster, F. (ed.) (2001) *Culture and Politics in the Information Age*, London: Routledge

Weimann, G. (2006) *Terror on the Internet: the new arena, the new challenges*, Washington, DC: United States Institute of Peace Press

Whittaker, D. (ed.) (2001) *The Terrorism Reader*, London: Routledge

Wikipedia (2007) 'Unix philosophy', available at http://en.wikipedia.org/wiki/Unix_philosophy, accessed May 2007

Williams, S. (2002) *Free as in Freedom: Richard Stallman's crusade for free software*, Sebastopol, CA: O'Reilly

Winner, L. (1977) *Autonomous Technology: technics-out-of-control as a theme in political thought*, Cambridge, Mass.: MIT Press

Yar, M. (2006) *Cybercrime and Society*, London: Sage

Index

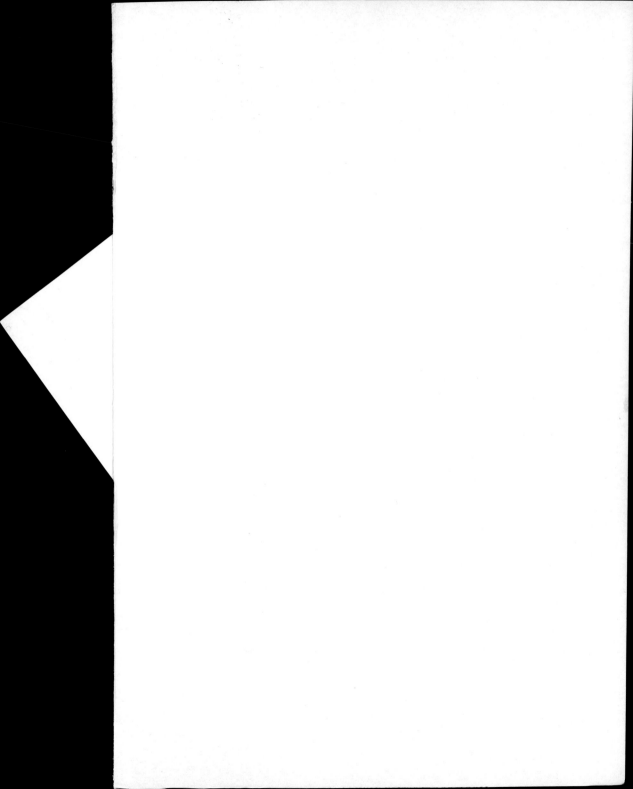

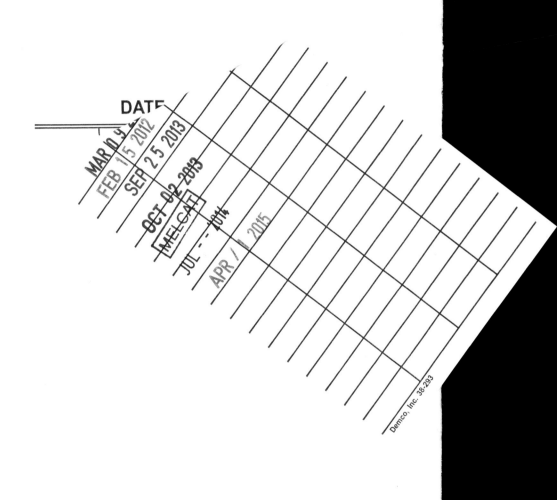